HYPNOCOP

HYPNOCOP

True-Life Cases of the N.Y.P.D.'s First Investigative Hypnotist

DETECTIVE SERGEANT
CHARLES DIGGETT
AND
WILLIAM C. MULLIGAN

Doubleday & Company, Inc., Garden City, New York
1982

The events described in this book are factual. Certain names, dates, and places have been changed to protect the people involved.

Library of Congress Cataloging in Publication Data

Diggett, Charles, 1927–
   Hypnocop: the true-life cases of the N.Y.P.D.'s first
investigative hypnotist.

   1. Diggett, Charles, 1927–   . 2. Police—New York
(N.Y.)—Biography. 3. Hypnotism and crime. 4. Criminal
investigation—New York (N.Y.)—Case studies. 5. New
York (N.Y.). Police Dept. I. Mulligan, William C.
II. Title.
HV7911.D53A34   363.2'54 [B]
AACR2
             ISBN: 0-385-17067-X
  Library of Congress Catalog Card Number 81–43142

TO THE WORLDWIDE COMMUNITY
OF LAW-ENFORCEMENT PERSONNEL

ACKNOWLEDGMENTS

In its metamorphosis from a body of experience to the permanence of the printed page, the realization of a book of this kind owes a debt of gratitude to a variety of people.

First and foremost, we would like to thank the men and women of the New York Police Department: Chief of Detectives James T. Sullivan for having the courage and foresight to stand behind a pioneering endeavor in the face of widespread resistance; the investigators who gave unstintingly of their time and recollections; Detective Millie Markman for her generous help in selecting cases and gathering tapes and transcripts, and Officer Mario Buda for untiringly transferring reel-to-reel recordings to cassette tapes.

A special tribute is owed the late Barbara Grant, a brilliant young literary agent who initiated the project and who was responsible for bringing its co-authors together. For carrying on her work with no less devotion, our heartfelt thanks go to Judy Bookman and Virginia Barber.

We are immeasurably appreciative of the professional expertise of the people at Doubleday, and would like to thank editors

Rafia Zafar for her early enthusiasm and support, Mary Trone for her expert guidance in the organization of the manuscript, and Susan Schwartz for her skillful final revisions.

For miraculously transcribing endless hours of near-incomprehensible recordings, we thank Nancy Huntley. And for their love and patience beyond the call of duty and their invaluable suggestions, we will be forever grateful to Lucille, Dennis, Marc, Eric, and Chris Diggett, the late William C. Mulligan, Sr., Eleanor Mulligan, Elvin McDonald, Marie Iervolino, Judy Savauge, and Joanne McKay.

CONTENTS

There is no need to run outside
For better seeing,
Nor to peer from a window. Rather abide
At the center of your being;
For the more you leave it, the less you learn.

Lao-tzu

1

A DETAIL CAPTURED

However tired a cliché the power of positive thinking may seem to some, the notion remains as provocative as always. In fact, its awesome validity looms ever larger as man delves deeper into the secrets of the mind. Many of history's noblest philosophies, from ancient Buddhism to modern-day Christian Science, are built on the firm foundation of positive thinking, and so is hypnosis. What one believes is, and if I can get subjects to truly *believe* that lost memories are within their grasp, then they *will* retrieve them.

In attempting to instill this faith, I consistently point out that the mind records all sensory input and stores it in the subconscious. Basically, this isn't out of line with current thought among behavioral scientists, but I never let on that the situation is far more complicated than the simple explanation would suggest. What the believing, hypnotized subject retrieves isn't always complete or accurate. Is this because the mind actually stores only selected details of what it experiences? Or is it because the hypnotically aided retrieval system isn't functioning optimally? There are no answers. We are still a long way from knowing how the brain operates in this capacity.

I don't think I can ever fully convey how astonished I am when a witness under hypnosis unearths bits and pieces that he couldn't possibly have remembered under ordinary circumstances. Yet at other times, when all systems are go and there doesn't seem to be any reason for subjects not to be able to reconstruct what they came face to face with, they draw a blank. In the more than four hundred criminal investigations I have worked on as a forensic hypnotist, I have found this to be especially true with license-plate numbers. A witness may have gotten a good look at the back of a car and the plate on it, and when hypnotized, may be able to tell me the color of the plate, the state, the year, perhaps, but an accurate reiteration of the numbers and letters is a rare exception. If I ask a subject, "When I count to three and tap on the table, call out the first number that comes to mind," he will often produce a number. But nine times out of ten, it isn't the one we are looking for. It may be his mother-in-law's or a plate he had on his own car some time in the past. In far too few cases, the witness remembered a part of the correct number, or the whole number with the digits interchanged. I don't know the reason for this near-consistent failure to register numbers and letters without error, but it may be that they are simply beyond the detail threshold, in most instances, of what the mind is willing to record.

As the New York Police Department's official hypnotist, it is my job to capture the forgotten detail, the crucial circumstance or bit of information that a witness' or victim's mind more than likely *has* recorded but is reluctant to relinquish to the conscious memory. Hypnosis' success rate in providing investigators with new and useful material has remained steady at about 60 per cent. The revelations that lie within this percentage are often all that is needed to tip the scales of justice in favor of the solution of a case. Many of the investigations I have been called in on, over the past five years, to perform my seeming magic, have been among the toughest to crack, and have involved some of the most bizarre crimes I have encountered in my twenty-nine years on the force.

At 6:30 P.M. on December 29, 1975, a powerful explosion ripped through one of the baggage claim areas at New York's La Guardia Airport, immediately killing eleven unsuspecting travelers and airline workers and injuring seventy more. The bombing's aftermath was a nightmare of rubble, shattered glass, and broken, charred bodies. Within an hour of the horrifying incident, the police received a telephone threat that a second bomb was in place and set to go off at any moment. But a massive search turned up nothing. There were no further explosions, and it was theorized that the false alarm had been an attempt to stall investigation proceedings and interrupt rescue operations.

Circumstances surrounding the act of destruction and mass homicide, including the anonymous phone call, gave an early indication that the bomb had been planted by organized insurgents. Weeks of backbreaking sifting of debris was undertaken in an effort to find at least one small clue leading to the perpetrators. The FBI was called in, and came up with some promising leads. A hypnotic interview provided a good description of a likely suspect, but to this day, no one has been arrested in connection with the case, and it remains unsolved.

An adult, male survivor informed the inspectors that he was suspicious of a man he had seen walking through the terminal a few minutes before the explosion. He said the individual caught his attention because of the way he carried his suitcase—resting flat on both arms, as if it contained a cake. He watched the man approach a wall of coin-operated lockers, open one, and deposit the case.

The investigators couldn't imagine why anyone would be holding a piece of luggage in so unusual a manner, unless, of course, it concealed a delicate mechanism of some kind, perhaps a time bomb. Since they had already determined that the blast had emanated from one of the baggage lockers, they were very interested in a description of the man with the suitcase. The witness couldn't remember anything about him, although he did recall a curious detail involving the terminal's support columns.

Each was marked with a number, and he thought he saw the suspect go to the bank of lockers positioned between columns one hundred and eleven and one hundred and twelve.

The investigators refrained from telling the witness that the explosion hadn't originated at this exact location. Hoping his memory had failed him, they called me in on the case, with the prospect that hypnosis might be able to elicit the correct location and uncover a buried recollection or two about the luggage-toting mystery man.

The witness was a very good subject. In a deep trance, he not only described the suspect's physical characteristics and every piece of clothing he was wearing but was able to remember the tiniest detail about the bag he was carrying—its size, color, material, type of handle, closures, and more.

I asked him, once again, to follow this person as he crossed the terminal floor.

"He's walking very smoothly, as if he doesn't want to jar the suitcase . . . but not very slowly. He's heading straight for the lockers."

"Is he at the lockers now?"

"Yes."

"Okay, freeze the action. Take a good look at the columns on each side of him, and call out the numbers you see on them."

"One hundred and eleven . . . and one hundred and ten!"

"Are you sure about those numbers?"

"Yes, I'm positive now. It's one-ten, not one-twelve. . . . I can see it clearly."

I glanced at the two investigators who were in the room with us. They both smiled and nodded. The witness hadn't seen their reactions. His eyes never opened.

The detectives were overjoyed with the results of the interview. Hypnosis had helped the survivor of the disaster hit the jackpot. His revised location was, indeed, where the bomb had gone off, and the investigators were now more confident that the man described, a true messenger of death, had been delivering an explosive device to its detonation site.

On a sunny June day in 1978, Officers Paul Alonzo and Arnold James had parked their patrol car out of sight of motorists, just

off Straight Path in Long Island's Suffolk County. Staked out to
net speeding offenders, the two had been clocking cars for hours
when a Mercury Cougar raced by. The vehicle was exceeding
the posted limit by a considerable margin, and the officers pulled
into the road in hot pursuit. When the reckless driver realized
that the police were bearing down on him, he accelerated, and
the chase was on. It continued through the countryside at death-
defying speeds, sometimes more than a hundred miles an hour.

Failing in their attempt to overtake the speeding vehicle, the
officers radioed for help. They reported their position—heading
down Straight Path in the direction of Sunrise Highway. The
call was answered by Detective Ronald Arelio, in the vicinity in
a squad car with Warrant Officer Mario DeLuca. The detective
thought he might make it to the intersection of Straight Path and
Sunrise in time to head off the speeding lawbreaker.

Lights flashing and siren blaring, the detective's car barreled
down Sunrise, weaving through traffic and running red lights. It
approached the Straight Path intersection seconds ahead of the
runaway Mercury. Just as the detective was about to slow the
squad car down, his path was crossed by an ice cream truck. He
hit the brakes, but it was too late. The car slammed into the
truck, and burst into flames.

The Mercury sailed through the intersection at breakneck
speed, and got away. Detective Arelio perished in the line of
duty. Officer DeLuca and the driver of the truck were critically
injured.

It was a short drive, two days later, from my home in Babylon
to Suffolk County police headquarters. I had been summoned to
hypnotize Officers Alonzo and James, in an effort to nail down a
solid description of the runaway Mercury. At that time, as far as
I know, forensic hypnosis had been used on Long Island only
once before, in a 1974 investigation into the kidnapping of a
Kings Point businessman. I wasn't involved in the case, and have
no knowledge of who the hypnotist was.

Both men responded well to the procedure. Although they had
never gotten close enough to be able to read the license on the
relatively old, banged-up vehicle, their heightened memories of it
were rich in detail. They reported that it was a 1967 or 1968
model Cougar with a black-vinyl top, that its green paint was

faded and its left side badly crumpled. They also remembered that the car's directional signals were made up of multiple lights that operated sequentially across the rear bumper.

An all-points bulletin was put out. Motorists were stopped and questioned at road blocks, and all 1967 through 1970 model Cougars fitting the officers' description were painstakingly traced. But the dragnet proved fruitless. The car and its homicidal driver were never found.

On a clear, brisk, October evening in 1979, a full moon illuminated the hills in Westchester County as Martin Kruger drove to the house he had once shared with Paula Kruger. The soft, romantic light reminded him of happier times with his wife of eight years. But they had been separated now for eleven months, and the thirty-year-old telephone company engineer was returning to his former residence to remove the last of his possessions. His estranged wife had grown tired of looking at his collection of phonograph records, and had asked him to come and take them away.

Martin arrived at the house at the prearranged time. He rang the bell and waited. There was no response. He leaned on the button longer the second time. Still no answer. He opened the storm door, and knocked as loud as he could, but to no avail.

"She must have gone out. Why did she do that? She knew what time I'd be getting here," he muttered to himself as he got into his car, and drove away.

Later that night, Martin reached Paula on the telephone. He asked her why she hadn't been home at eight o'clock when he had said he would be coming over.

"The door wasn't locked," Paula replied. "You should have tried it. Don't you remember, I told you if I wasn't there, to go in."

"Okay, I'll come by again on Thursday at the same time. Is that all right?"

"Fine."

Two days later, Martin was once more at the house ringing the bell. After waiting a respectful length of time, he tried the door. It wasn't locked. He walked in and flipped on the hall light, but nothing happened. He made his way in the dark toward the dining room where his records were. Before he got there, he heard a sound from somewhere behind him. He spun around, and was just beginning to discern movement in the darkness when suddenly a sharp crack reverberated violently within his skull. Stunned and in excruciating pain, Martin slumped to the floor. He was conscious, though hopelessly dazed.

"Please help me stand up," he said in his confusion.

He was obligingly given a hand, but no sooner had he been propped up than his assailant took another swing with his baseball bat, and brought it down on Martin's head again.

"What did I do to deserve this?" he thought. He still hadn't lost consciousness, but got the message this time, and lay motionless in a heap on the floor.

"What're we gonna do now?" he heard a male voice say.

"I think it's time to shoot him," another answered.

Martin refused to believe what the man said. "Surely these characters are only burglars. If I just lie here, without making a move, they'll go away."

He heard one of the men walk to another room. When he came back, he was dragging something across the floor. Martin felt what seemed to be a soft cloth brushing the side of his face. The man wrapped the heavy quilt around the pistol he was holding, and put the barrel to the back of Martin's head.

The defenseless victim heard a loud pop, followed by a ringing in his left ear. He knew he had been shot, but, miraculously, he was still alive. He wasn't even unconscious. At least he *thought* he was alive and conscious. He felt something running down the side of his neck.

"It must be blood." With all the control he could muster, he remained as still as he had before.

One of the thugs took hold of his left wrist. "I think he's dead."

The other grabbed the right one. "Yeah, you're right, Joe. He *is* dead."

"Jesus Christ, I'm dead! I don't feel like I am, but I must be if I don't have a pulse," Martin reasoned. "Can I move? I'd better not try."

"What're we gonna do with him, Joe?"

"We have to get him out of Westchester."

"What about the blood on the floor?"

"Don't worry, that's not our problem. That's *her* problem."

They wrapped the quilt around Martin's "lifeless" body, carried it out to his own car, and tossed it in the trunk. One of the men got behind the wheel, while the other jumped into the car that had brought the two to the house. With Martin going steady with a spare tire in the lead car, they drove for about twenty minutes to a deserted junkyard in the Bronx. They hurled Martin's "body" onto a pile of rubble near his parked car, and sped away in their own vehicle.

Martin lay there motionless, hurting all over. "Should I try to move? No, I'd better wait a few minutes."

It was a wise decision. The perpetrators remembered the quilt. They came back, pulled it off the victim, and drove away again. Martin listened for the sound of the engine fading in the distance. Even after it disappeared, he remained absolutely still for about ten minutes more. Then he discovered, to his great relief, that he could move; he wasn't dead. He climbed into the car and raced to his girl friend Anne's house. He searched for a police car on the way, but saw no sign of one.

When Anne opened the door, she gasped. The sight of her lover standing there with blood streaming down his face was worse than any nightmare she could remember. She rushed Martin to the county hospital.

The doctor on duty in the emergency room was skeptical of the man's incredible story. A New York City detective happened to be there on another case, and overheard the victim claiming to have been clobbered on the head and then shot. The detective looked at the doctor disbelievingly.

"Don't listen to him," the physician advised the lawman. "He's crazy."

But before the detective left, he got Martin to assure him that he would call the Westchester police, and tell them about the assault.

Not until the attending physician took X-rays of Martin's skull to determine if it had been fractured, did he finally believe his account of having been shot. There was no mistaking the clear X-ray image of a bullet lodged just behind Martin's left ear. A fraction of an inch one way or the other, and the victim wouldn't have survived.

The investigation of the implausible attempted homicide began the next day. After listening to Martin's incredible tale, the police labeled Paula Kruger a prime suspect. It would seem that she had set up her estranged husband, luring him to the house under the pretext that he reclaim the last of his belongings, meanwhile arranging with hired killers to man the trap she had laid. The investigators acquired a likely motive when Martin told them that Paula was still the beneficiary of a one-hundred-thousand-dollar insurance policy on his life.

In the pursuit of evidence linking Paula with the unsuccessful assassins, the lawmen were very much interested in a telephone conversation her estranged husband had had with her some weeks before the incident. Martin explained that his wife had called to ask for a favor.

"I have this friend who's willing to loan me a thousand dollars, Martin. With that, I could go to Mexico, get a divorce, and settle this whole thing."

"Sounds good to me."

"The only problem is, I've mislaid his telephone number, and it's unlisted. Do you think you could get it for me?"

Paula took it for granted that, as a phone company employee, Martin had access to unpublished listings. He agreed to try, and Paula gave him the man's name.

Martin succeeded in procuring the information, and passed it on to Paula. But when he tried to remember the name or number for the police, the only thing that came to mind was a first name —Joe.

Realizing that this was what the victim had overheard one of his assailants call the other, the detectives were hopeful of establishing a connection. They came up with the idea of using hypnosis to jog their prize witness' memory. With the approval of my commanding officer, I went off to Westchester to hypnotize the attempted murder victim.

Somewhat distracted by his injuries, Martin proved to be a rather difficult subject. He seemed to be recovering all right, but was bothered by some discomfort and a substantial hearing loss in the ear the bullet was still lodged behind. Because of the danger involved, there had been no attempt to remove the projectile, and, as far as I know, it is still there.

Despite the less-than-ideal circumstances, I succeeded in coaxing Martin into a medium-level trance. Although the investigators had hoped for more, they were grateful for the three digits of the telephone exchange and the first two letters of the suspect's last name that hypnosis ultimately extracted from the subject's subconscious. It was a tribute to the detectives' resourcefulness that they were able to piece together a whole name and number from the morsel of additional material I succeeded in securing for them.

The named man's partner-in-crime was identified, and it was revealed that the two were acquaintances of Roger Duvall, Paula's paramour at the time. The investigators surmised that he and Paula had conspired to do away with Martin, and had made a pact with the alleged hit men.

Soon after being questioned by the police about her involvement in the case, Paula attempted suicide by taking an overdose of sleeping pills, then took refuge in the psychiatric unit of the local general hospital. Fully recovered from the ordeal, she was brought to trial in August 1980. On the fourth day, the defendant, in tears, interrupted the proceedings to plead guilty to attempted murder in the second degree. In the hushed courtroom, she read aloud a statement that her attorney had prepared for her.

"I asked my husband to meet me alone in our . . . home, knowing two men were there who would beat, shoot, and kill him. The motive of this crime was to obtain life insurance proceeds on the life of Martin Kruger."

Roger Duvall surrendered himself to the police in September 1980, and was held on fifty thousand dollars' bail. In the same month, the alleged hit men were arrested. One of the two is scheduled for trial at this writing, and the other has co-operated with the prosecution in exchange for bargaining a plea. Paula Kruger is awaiting sentencing, pending the outcome of the trials of her three co-conspirators.

On the second floor of Transit Authority headquarters at 370 Jay Street in Brooklyn is a large space where all revenue collected from city buses and subway change booths is assembled and counted. Collating cubicles line the periphery of the room, while a cagelike structure containing three enormous vaults dominates the center. Every evening, the day's sorted and bundled currency is locked safely away until the following morning, when it is carted to the bank. A security guard at each of the only two accesses to the area plus closed-circuit television cameras keep all work operations and comings and goings under twenty-four-hour surveillance.

It would appear that every precaution imaginable has been taken to make thievery a virtual impossibility. Yet on July 17, 1979, six hundred thousand dollars—sixty bundles of ten-dollar bills, a thousand bills per bundle—disappeared from one of the safes, right under the noses of twenty-five to thirty employees.

Sixteen-year veteran of the Transit Authority police, Detective Jim Brown, and his partner, Detective Peter Devine, with the assistance of Detectives Joe Robinson and Joe Monahan of the New York police's Major Case Squad, were in charge of investigating the most baffling crime of their careers. As far as any of the TA workers knew, all the money in one of the vaults had been accounted for when it was locked up at the end of the day on Friday. But when it was opened on Monday morning, it was discovered that half the money that should have been in it was gone.

There were no signs of forced entry, and the investigators theorized that the theft was an inside job. Since it would have been impossible for either the security guards or anyone else to open the safe during the weekend without being detected, the job had to have been pulled off before the safe was closed and all employees left for the day on Friday. But six hundred thousand dollars in ten-dollar bills is a hefty amount of currency. Indeed, it comprises a three-foot-square block weighing one hundred and twenty pounds, unwieldy to say the least, and the detectives hadn't a clue as to how it could have been secreted from the room in full view of the guards and TA staff.

Most of the counters and supervisors working in the revenue room had been doing the same job for thirty or forty years. They were trusted and conscientious employees, nonetheless, victims of monotonous routine. They sorted and collated for the most part with practiced automation, and when asked by the investigators what they were doing or where they had been in the room at specific times of the day, it was impossible for them to remember anything beyond their all-too-familiar tasks. As far as they were concerned, nothing out of the ordinary seemed to have taken place.

I first met Jim Brown at a training session. He was impressed by the possibilities of forensic hypnosis, and, predating the safe heist, we had worked together on a number of cases. He figured that a telling bit of information might be brought out from the backs of some of the TA employees' minds if they were hypnotized. He came to my office with ten of the workers in tow.

The sessions proved to be an exhausting, all-day undertaking, but not without reward. In fact, it was utterly fascinating to see how easily and accurately some of the more hypnotically suggestible employees were able to pinpoint their activities as soon as they were put into a trance. From the information I was able to retrieve, the investigators deduced that all the money was intact in the safe at 5:45 P.M. and that half of it was gone at 5:50 P.M. This was a remarkable revelation, especially considering the fact that every worker innocent of wrongdoing went home that evening with no *conscious* awareness of anything having been amiss. And the indication of the quicker-than-the-eye swiftness with which the caper was pulled off was not all that hypnosis helped uncover. Additional pertinent material surfaced for the detectives' scrutiny. Unfortunately, I am not free to divulge what it was because, at this point, more than two years after the theft, the case is still under investigation.

If and when the robbery is solved, I can say with confidence that hypnosis was essential to its solution. Jim's words to me shortly after the interviews tell the story very well.

"Hypnosis gave us an enormous amount of information that we wouldn't have gotten otherwise. I was really impressed. Where people were and what they were doing at certain times is important to the case. When we questioned them about this, they didn't have any idea what time it was when they performed various tasks. But hypnosis revealed that their subconscious minds were very much aware of the clock. And when you asked them to look at it while they were under, they told you what it read, even though on that afternoon, they weren't conscious of noticing the time. This and other information that came up under hypnosis gave us some very direct leads."

The investigation remains one of the most fascinating in the annals of crime. Besides hypnosis, every existing forensic tool has been called into play, including the use of sodium pentothal, polygraph tests, and psychic consultation. As a result, the investigators are now fairly certain which two or three individuals masterminded the heist. Arrests can be made only when and if the criminals spend some of the money, an informant drops a dime to claim the twenty-five-thousand-dollar reward, one of the perpetrators cracks, or the lawmen secure further evidence that will hold up in court. Jim Brown is ever optimistic that the case will be resolved.

December 19, 1978, was a freezing, dark day on New York's Staten Island. Nonetheless, bundled up against the chill, Louise Murphy was at work as usual at the service station managed by her husband. In her mid-twenties and the mother of three small children, Louise put in regular hours every day at the station, pumping gas and performing other light chores to relieve her husband of some of his heavy work load.

She had just finished topping off a customer's tank, and was digging into her pocket for change, when she noticed a black Cadillac pull up to one of the pumps. The driver jumped out, and without waiting for an attendant, grabbed the line, and started pumping his own gas.

"He's certainly in a big hurry," Louise said to herself. She wondered if the man was a doctor or a medical technician of some kind. He was wearing a long, white lab coat.

"Are you going to fill 'er up?" she asked, as she approached the car.

The man stared at her, and said nothing.

"Are you going to fill the tank?" This time Louise's voice had a definite edge to it. She was more than a little annoyed with the man for presuming he was at a self-service station. Besides, there was a problem with the pump he was using. It had a habit of not turning off unless you knew exactly how to manipulate it. Louise wanted to warn him about this. But he still refused to speak, so she just stood by, waiting for the gas to spill on the ground.

She noticed that the car was carrying close to a full load. Its four passengers, all male, and the driver seemed agitated about something. One of the men in the back seat handed Louise a dollar, and asked her to get him a pack of cigarettes. She obliged, and when she came back, the impatient gas jockey was returning the fuel nozzle to its cradle.

"I guess he figured out how to turn it off," she thought.

The meter read fifteen dollars. The man handed Louise a twenty. She fumbled through a roll of bills for a five, and when she finally came up with one, the driver snatched it from her hand. He was obviously in a hurry, and in a huff over having to wait even a few seconds for change. He slid behind the wheel, and roared out of the station. Remembering her husband's admonition about bills larger than a ten, Louise quickly grabbed a pencil. She had just enough time to scratch the license number on the twenty as the car pulled away.

About forty-five minutes later and two miles from the station, a Wells Fargo truck parked in front of a delicatessen. The armored vehicle was transporting a cache of almost two and a half million dollars to the Federal Reserve Bank in Manhattan. It was lunchtime, and the driver and two security guards escorting the haul of cold currency had stopped to pick up some sandwiches.

Leaving the driver behind the wheel, the two guards got out of the truck, paying little attention either to the Cadillac parked behind them or the three men, one wearing a lab coat, who went ahead of them into the store. The pair of armed security officers joined the threesome and others in line at the counter.

What followed was so swift that it was over before the guards had time to react. Two of the men jumped off the line, whipped out handguns, and placed them at the guards' heads. The cold metal dug into the stunned security men's scalps as they raised their hands in compliance with the gunmen's orders. A woman behind the counter screamed, but stopped abruptly when the third man produced a sawed-off shotgun from under his white coat, and leveled the menacing-looking weapon at her. As he kept the few customers and employees in the store covered, the other two removed the guards' pistols from their holsters, and shunted the pair to a back room. The frightened customers and workers were herded into the same area. The guards were handcuffed, but not before one of them, in response to his captors' demands, surrendered the keys that unlocked the truck.

While the seizure of the delicatessen was underway, a quieter but no less threatening scenario was unfolding outside. A fourth member of the ambush team left the Cadillac and walked over to the armored truck.

"Hey, buddy, you know this front tire here is losing air."

"It is? Thanks for telling me." The Wells Fargo driver got out of the truck and bent down to examine the tire. Suddenly he felt something hard pressed against the small of his back.

"Don't make a sound, and don't move, or you're getting this right through your gut." The gang member's gun served him as well concealed in his pocket as it would have brandished in the open.

At that moment, the three who had been in the store emerged and rushed over to the truck. One of them quickly unlocked the back doors and jumped inside, followed by another. The driver's captor, after brutally shoving his charge in ahead of him, also boarded the armored cargo hold. As soon as the character in the white coat had locked the doors behind his cohorts and their hostage, he climbed into the cab and drove the criminal- and treasure-laden truck away. The Cadillac, with the fifth and last hood at the wheel, trailed close behind.

In a secluded spot about three blocks from the deli, all hands worked feverishly to transfer the bags of plunder—two million, two hundred and forty-seven thousand dollars' worth, to be exact—to the waiting Cadillac. They didn't bother lugging some tens of thousands of dollars more in coins. These were left behind to keep the bound and gagged driver company.

When Louise Murphy heard the first news reports of the mammoth heist, she immediately called the police. She had thought there was something sinister about that group of men, and now her suspicions were confirmed. The white lab coat and the black Cadillac mentioned in the bulletin were the tip-offs. Louise was sure that the men she had dealt with and the robbers were one and the same.

The Staten Island police passed the promising lead on to the Major Case Squad at central headquarters in Manhattan. In collaboration with the Federal Bureau of Investigation, this unit was in charge of tracking down the perpetrators. The Major Case Squad is an elite group of highly experienced detectives who are normally assigned crimes of far-reaching implication, such as bank robberies and assassinations or kidnappings of dignitaries and government officials. The squad maintains a branch in the Federal Building, and is the only law-enforcement unit in the country that works directly with the FBI on a regular basis.

Under the command of the squad's Lieutenant Carrol, the investigation focused initially on the security guards and innocent bystanders accosted in the delicatessen. The victims supplied descriptions of some of the men, and reported that the getaway car was a black Cadillac, possibly a 1974 or 1975 model. No one could be sure. Unfortunately, the vehicle's license had escaped everyone's notice.

Two of the investigators on the case went to the service station to talk to Louise. The young woman gave them descriptions of three of the men, including the one in the lab coat, and said she was certain that the car was a 1974 Cadillac. Her conviction was based on the fact that the vehicle looked exactly like her brother's, of the same year and make. When she told the detectives she had written the license number on the bill she was paid with, naturally they were encouraged. Asked if she had any idea what the number was, Louise searched her mind, but recalled only that the plate was from New Jersey. As far as the number was concerned, her memory refused to co-operate.

Thanks to the excellent work of the case's investigative team, the crucial twenty-dollar bill was found. The numbers and letters scribbled on it, five, two, eight, G, H, I, the state, and—with the speculation that the plates were unexpired—the current year, 1978, were fed into the Department of Motor Vehicles' computer. The electronic marvel spewed out the name and address of a New Jersey resident. According to the all-knowing memory banks, the owner of the plate lived in a quiet, suburban community.

Two investigators went, unannounced, to the indicated address. The house was a typical family residence, not at all the kind of place they expected to find criminals holed up in. A friendly, middle-aged man appeared at the door. The detectives identified themselves, and asked the man if he would mind answering a few questions.

"No, I'd be glad to. Come inside."

"Are you familiar with automobile license number five, two, eight, G, H, I?" one of the two inquired.

"Yes, I am."

"Is it on your car at the present time?"

"No, I have two plates with that number, and they're in the basement."

"May we see them?"

"Sure, come with me."

The detectives stared at the rectangular sheets of metal. They bore the number they were looking for, all right, but the men's finely honed instincts told them they had reached a dead end. The person they were dealing with gave every indication of being a law-abiding citizen. It was highly unlikely that he had had anything to do with the holdup.

Follow-up investigation substantiated the detectives' intuition. The owner was what he had appeared to be, an honest individual with a clean record. The lawmen could only conclude that Louise had made a mistake in copying the number. Not defeated yet, they went back to the witness. Without revealing what they had concluded was written on the bill, they asked the young woman once more to try to remember what the plate number was. After some very hard thinking, she said she thought the first two numbers were five and two, but that was all she could come up with.

At this point in the investigation, I was contacted by Detective Joe Robinson. Joe is a top-notch investigator with twenty-five years' experience as a detective. He has been with the MC Squad since its inception, and had requested my participation as a hypnotist on a couple of cases prior to this one. Joe was familiar with hypnosis' capabilities, and had a hunch it was the catalyst needed to trigger the release of that obstinate series of numbers and letters from Louise's mind.

When I met at the Major Case offices with Joe, another investigator, an FBI agent, and the witness, I was mulling over past failures to retrieve complete license numbers, and had grave doubts that this interview would prove to be one of the rare exceptions.

After Louise's reiteration—still without a complete license number—of her conscious recollections of the incident, the hypnotic interview got off to a good start. An exceptionally responsive subject for the first time out, she went into a deep trance. Her descriptions of three of the hoods, especially the one outfitted in the lab coat, were amazingly complete. While I had her looking with her mind's eye at the Cadillac, waiting for the driver to finish pumping gas, I asked if she could see the car's license plate.

"Yes, I can see the front plate. . . . It's attached to the bumper loosely with wires, as if it isn't permanent."

This was new and encouraging information to everyone in the room. My hopes were up.

"What are the numbers on the plate, Louise? . . . Take your time and look at the license. You can see those numbers. Tell us what they are."

"I can't really see them. . . . I think, maybe, five . . . two . . . no, that's all I remember. . . . Wait a minute. . . . There's a small orange sticker in the corner of the plate. It says '74 on it."

"Are you sure about that, Louise?"

"Yes, I didn't remember it before, but now I can see it."

If accurate, this fact provided the investigators with the heretofore undisclosed information that the criminals were driving around with expired plates. It might seem foolish of them to be doing so, but it wouldn't be unusual.

I asked the subject to breathe deeply, and offered suggestions of calmness and relaxation. Then I told her to move up to the time when the car was pulling away from the station, when she was recording the license on the bill.

"You're writing those numbers down now, Louise. See the bill in your hand, and watch the pencil moving across the paper. . . . I'm going to count to three, and when I do, I'll hit the table here with my hand. As soon as you hear that sound, I want you to call out the numbers as quickly as you can. . . . One . . . two . . . three. . . ."

I slapped the table hard, with an open hand.

"Five, two, eight . . . G, H, T!"

The subject's outburst caught me by surprise, as it did the investigators. I hadn't really expected her to produce a complete number.

"Do those numbers and letters feel right to you, Louise?"

"Yes, they do. . . . I'm really amazed."

"You're sure they're not from a plate belonging to you or a member of your family?"

"Yes, I'm positive. Five, two, eight, G, H, T is what I wrote down."

As soon as I returned Louise to normal consciousness, one of the investigators showed her the twenty-dollar bill.

"Look at what's written here, Louise—five, two, eight, G, H, *I*. But under hypnosis you said it was five, two, eight, G, H, *T*. Now which is it?"

"That's not an I. It's the way I make a T. Besides, did you ever try to write on a bill while holding it in the palm of your hand?"

The investigators came away from the interview with a new number to trace. Of course, they would have been off on another wild goose chase if it weren't for Louise's hypnotically aided recollection of the orange sticker. This little detail concerning the expired year made all the difference in the world. The FBI agent in attendance at the hypnosis session was a New Jersey resident, and he was of the opinion that markers of this kind were not in use in 1974. But when he checked into it, he discovered, sure enough, they were required on some plates, and they *were* orange.

The investigators' thoroughness in their determination to connect the license to an owner launched them on a countrywide chase. The Cadillac and the plates originally belonged to a New Jersey rental company, which sent the car to an affiliate on the West Coast. Damaged in an accident, the vehicle was sent back to Jersey to be repaired. Because the rental company was unwilling to pay the high cost of the repairs, it relinquished ownership to the body shop, which in turn sold the car to an automobile wholesaler in the Bronx.

"The people at the repair company," Joe Robinson told me, "insisted that the car and the plates went to the wholesaler. They said that when they sell a car, everything goes with it. They'd never take the plates off. But when we went to the company in the Bronx, the people there claimed that they got the car, but no plates. With a little digging into the background of this place, we came up with mob connections. That's how we were able to link the holdup to organized crime. The witness you hypnotized was very helpful in this case."

While the mazelike trail of ownerships was being pursued, the car was found abandoned. Its plates had been removed, but fingerprints taken from it put the investigators onto a suspect who fit Louise's description of the hood in the white coat perfectly. The man was identified, and it turned out he had a history of mob involvement.

With an irony befitting the operatic sweep of the months-long investigation that led to the suspect, he was arrested at the posh Windows on the World restaurant at the top of the World Trade Center minutes before his wedding was to take place.

2

A FACE REVEALED

The towers of Manhattan fill the horizon to the west, looming above the squat buildings and decaying streets of the Queens County industrial district. The glamour the skyline promises isn't to be found here. This is a world of smokestacks, empty lots, and corner luncheonettes frequented by blue-collar workers, and Twenty-first Street runs through the heart of this somber cityscape. Warehouses and small factories line its crumbling roadbed, presided over by the elevated tracks of the IRT Subway. One building, covered with years of soot and grime, bears a sign, "L. H. Harrison Manufacturing Company."

At 1:50 P.M. on Friday, June 22, 1979, Twenty-first Street was silent. The morning's din of machinery, of trucks arriving and departing, loading and unloading, had given way to the eerie quiet of lunch break. The street was deserted, save for a lone figure who now emerged, soundlessly, from the shadow of the el.

He reached into his jacket pocket, pulled something out, and stretched it down over his head. A knitted ski mask gave him the anonymous, if not menacing, appearance he had chosen for the job at hand. He walked hurriedly toward the Harrison Company warehouse and was soon swallowed by the darkness inside the freight entrance.

Moments later, a sudden report echoed down the corridor of el columns. The explosion's staccato repercussions traveled for blocks, but to the workers within earshot, the sound passed for the familiar backfiring of a truck. It would have been unlikely for them to suspect that what they had heard was the firing of a gun, and that it had come from within the Harrison warehouse.

A second shot followed minutes behind the first. Before its last reverberation sounded, the intruder reappeared at the warehouse entry carrying a handgun, but with his mask pulled up, revealing part of his face. He paused momentarily to adjust the mask, slipped the gun into a pocket, and began to run. He kept glancing back over his shoulder. In a flash, he disappeared around the corner.

Inside the building, Frank Pallermo pressed the button that activated the warehouse's huge overhead metal door, to seal off the cavernous space from further intrusion. As the electric motors sprang into action and before the door had clanged shut, the thirty-seven-year-old worker stumbled in the direction of the office, a small room in a corner of the warehouse.

"Christ, I hope the bastard doesn't come back," he muttered to himself. A sharp pain burned at the point behind his shoulder where a single bullet had found its mark. Blood oozed from the wound as Frank measured his failing strength against the four or five yards separating him from the office and the telephone.

He stopped at the doorway to a small storeroom adjoining the office and glanced inside. He was confronted with the gruesome sight of a man sprawled on the floor in a pool of blood. His co-worker, Ralph Kovacs, hadn't moved an inch since that awful moment when Frank first saw him there among the barrels and crates.

"He must be dead."

A wave of nausea washed over him as he remembered suddenly how narrowly he had missed the same fate. He imagined himself lying there next to Ralph, but erased the thought by directing his attention to John Terry. He was the purchasing agent and the only other worker Frank knew to be in the building.

"Where the hell is John?" he barked in utter frustration.

As soon as the perpetrator had run from the building, Frank had cried out for help, hoping that John would respond. But the man was in a closed room at the opposite end of the warehouse. Aside from some muffled sounds that easily could have been mistaken for a truck or a couple of firecrackers, he was completely unaware of the assault.

Finally, when Ralph had given up hope that there was anyone there who could help him, he saw John running toward him from the other end of the building.

"What's wrong? What happened?" John blurted out as he caught his breath.

"Ralph was shot. . . . He's on the floor. . . . I'm wounded," Frank managed between gulps of air, conveying the alarming facts in as few words as possible.

After John was assured that the entrance to the building was secure, he helped Frank into the office. The injured man's first concern was to report the incident to his employers. As he picked up the phone to call the Harrison Company's main office, John dashed to another phone at the far end of the warehouse and dialed 911.

Police officers John McCabee and Tony Bruno were cruising the area in a patrol car when the homicide report was dispatched over the radio. They sped to the scene of the crime. After surveying the situation, they confirmed the fact that Ralph Kovacs was beyond help. The single squeeze of a trigger had snatched the twenty-eight-year-old from his wife and two young children forever.

It was obvious to the two patrolmen that Frank Pallermo was in need of medical attention fast, but the ambulance his fellow worker had requested still hadn't arrived. One of the officers put out an emergency call on the car radio, bearing down with the full force of his authority in demanding immediate action. In a matter of minutes, an ambulance appeared. Frank was administered to and then rushed to Elmhurst General Hospital.

After examining Frank's X-rays, the doctors decided not to remove the bullet at that time. It was lodged dangerously close to the victim's spinal column. The wound was dressed and Frank was sent home.

The investigation of the cold-blooded assault and homicide fell into the hands of Detective Kevin McLaughlin of Queens's 108th Precinct. Then thirty-seven years old, married and the father of two, McLaughlin was a resourceful and dedicated officer of the law. His keen investigative sense had been honed by sixteen years' experience on the force. For the warehouse homicide assignment, he was going to have to dig deeply into his trusty bag of professional skills.

The few pieces of evidence retrieved at the warehouse didn't give McLaughlin much to go on: some partial prints proved to be too blurred to be of any use; a wristwatch and a pair of shattered eyeglasses—both without prints and neither belonging to any of the Harrison employees—were found on the floor, close to where the assaults took place. And that was it. Clearly, the only promising lead hinged on the crime's sole witness and survivor, Frank Pallermo, and his capacity to recall as many details as possible about the incident and the mysterious masked perpetrator.

The detective questioned Frank just hours after he had gotten home from the hospital. Despite the assault victim's shattered physical and emotional state, the afternoon's occurrences were emblazoned in his mind. McLaughlin asked him where he was when he first saw his assailant and what happened from that point on.

"I was just finishing eating my lunch in the warehouse office," Frank replied. "Ralph was there with me. A call came in from the main office and Ralph answered it. I just happened to get up from the chair where I was sitting. Then out of a clear blue sky, this fellow came through the door in a ski mask, pointing a gun. The guy didn't say it was a holdup or anything. He just kept pointing the gun and he was shaking. Then I remember Ralph stepping toward the guy and the next thing I knew, the gun went off. Ralph just froze on his feet. Right away, the guy ran out into the main part of the warehouse and I ran the same way after him. But he disappeared. I didn't see him anywhere. I ran toward the main entrance, and when I got in front of the doorway to the storeroom next to the office, the guy jumped from behind some cartons. He pointed the gun at me, and told me to 'lay down next to your friend.' As I walked into the storeroom, I saw Ralph already on the floor. I knew this guy was going to shoot me, too. I was scared, but I thought to myself, 'What have I got to lose?' So I grabbed for his gun, and that's when I got into a wrestle with him. I hit him a few times and he hit me in the head with the butt of the gun. I got his mask off part ways. Then he shot me in the back near my neck. After that, he took off, ran out the door and across the street. That was the last I saw of him."

"Now there's one thing I'm confused about," McLaughlin responded. "When the suspect came in, you said Ralph went toward him, and he shot Ralph?"

"Yeah, that's when I heard a shot go off."

"Then you said you went toward the front and ran into the suspect again, right?"

"Right."

"And Ralph was on the floor there?"

"Right, he was on the floor."

"So evidently when he got shot he didn't fall down?"

"No, he didn't fall down at that spot. He was lying maybe twenty, twenty-five feet away, in the storeroom next to the office. After he was shot, he must've gone through the door connecting the two rooms."

"He was shot only that one time?"

"As far as I know, yes. . . . I didn't hear any other shot."

"What did the gun look like?"

"It was a pistol, silver, and it had a white handle on it."

"Besides the gun, what else did you notice about this man?"

"He had the ski mask on. I couldn't see his face."

"About how tall was he?"

"He was, I'd say, under six feet, at the most."

"Was he taller than you?"

"I'd say, just a little taller than me."

"How tall are you?"

137124

"About five-ten, five-eleven."

"So he was somewhere between five-eleven and six feet?"

"Six feet, no more."

"What was his build?"

"Medium, I'd say, medium build. He wasn't that big."

"And what was he wearing?"

"The ski mask was sort of a dark blue color. And around the outline of the eyes there was red, green around the mouth. He had on a white jacket with a zipper in the front. And the pants were dark, exactly what color I couldn't really tell."

"Was there anything on the jacket, any lettering or patches?"

"No, I didn't see anything on the jacket at all."

"And what did he have under it?"

"It was zippered up. I couldn't see."

"Did you see his lips and his teeth when you pulled the mask up?"

"Vaguely, really . . . vaguely, you know?"

"Is there anything else you can recall about him?"

"Something unusual you mean? Like I say, when he came in . . . The mask was on him all the time. Really, I couldn't see much. But I don't think he was anybody who was ever in the warehouse before."

McLaughlin kept at it, in pursuit of a description of the killer. He succeeded in establishing that the man's complexion was, "sort of like Muhammad Ali's," but he couldn't get the witness/victim to describe his assailant's features. He reasoned that, in the struggle, Frank couldn't have gotten more than a split-second look at the face under the mask. There was his state of mind at the time to consider. He certainly looked drained and exhausted at the end of the interrogation. The disappointed investigator thanked Frank for his co-operation and wished him a rapid recovery. He also asked him to give him a call if he remembered anything more, and to remain available for further questioning.

McLaughlin's efforts to determine if anyone had seen the suspect approaching or leaving the premises yielded nothing. His canvassing included every factory in the area, a bakery shop and diner at the end of the block, and even the bus drivers who worked the route that passed the warehouse. Nobody remembered seeing or hearing anything. The thorough investigator was discovering nothing more than the fact that his suspect had shrewdly picked a time when he knew the streets and factories would be relatively empty.

The next day, the detective again focused his attention on his prize witness. He brought Frank over to the Bureau of Criminal Investigation (BCI), housed in New York's central police headquarters at One Police Plaza in downtown Manhattan, and had him look through hundreds of pictures from the BCI's file of suspected and convicted offenders. The results were negative. Although Frank thought he would remember his attacker's face if he saw it again, he was unable to find it in his careful search through piles of mug shots.

More determined than discouraged, McLaughlin started to check old robberies, hoping to come across the same ski-mask-and-silver-revolver *modus operandi*, or one similar to it. He discovered a rash of warehouse robberies in his precinct and in the 114th in Astoria over a two-year period prior to the homicide. In each, the same MO was repeated: A man would come in looking for a job. He would be told there was nothing available and would respond by pulling out a silver, .22-caliber handgun. The records showed that, in three of the cases, the perpetrator wore a ski mask.

With his first solid lead under his belt, McLaughlin felt a rush of encouragement. The prospect of putting away an obvious menace to society excited him. Taking the glasses and watch found at the Harrison Company, he went to a warehouse that had been robbed two months before. The surviving victim described the robbery's circumstances.

"The worker told me," McLaughlin remembered, "that this guy, the perpetrator, had glasses on, and he came in looking for a job. He gave some fictitious name and claimed to be working at a Burger King on Astoria Boulevard. This turned out not to be true. After they took down his phony name, the guy left.

"He then returns a couple of minutes later without the glasses on. He pulls out a silver pistol, a small gun, and says, 'Give me the money.' The witness leads him to a cage with a safe in it. As he gets to the cage, he turns around and the guy now has on a dark blue ski mask. So, in turn, this witness saw three versions of the same individual: without glasses, with glasses, and with the ski mask. He couldn't identify him because his whole train of thought had been thrown off.

"If you look at it," the detective went on, "this perp was pretty devious. That was the part that threw me because when I showed the witness the glasses, he said, 'Those are the glasses.' But he couldn't remember what the guy looked like, even though he did recall that he saw him outfitted three different ways. As a matter of fact, the perp was going to take his watch. He had already given him the money, and he said, 'Don't take my watch. It's a family heirloom. I'll give you anything but not my watch.' The guy said, 'All right, you can keep it.'

"The witness told me the suspect was soft-spoken, very calm, not at all nervous. At the time of the homicide, he was shaking and seemed very tense."

For the first time, the usually undaunted Irishman began to have grave doubts about ever solving the case. It was a tough one. He was going over what little material he had one more time when he suddenly remembered something he had heard about—hypnosis. One of the detectives he worked with had mentioned the department's newly established Hypnosis Unit, and how a witness or victim, once hypnotized, was purported to be able to remember what took place, what he saw or heard, in greater detail—something about the subconscious.

It didn't take McLaughlin long to realize that the mere mention of hypnosis provoked all kinds of smirks and snide remarks among many of the officers in his precinct, especially the more hard-line, tradition-bound types. He, too, was skeptical, but he figured, "Maybe there was something in Frank's subconscious that was being held back from me, something that might help—anything, a scar on the guy's face, a mole, an earring in his ear, anything at all that would give me a lead. I had nothing at that point. I was going absolutely nowhere. It was a long shot, but I even had hopes that hypnosis might help Frank remember enough to give us a composite sketch."

The detective had reached a decision. He would give hypnosis a try. He told Frank what he was planning and made sure the man knew what he was getting into. Frank had never been hypnotized before, but agreed to the procedure.

When the phone rang early on a Monday in June of '79, I answered it in the usual manner: "Sergeant Diggett, Hypnosis Unit." The caller introduced himself as Kevin McLaughlin of the 108th PDU, and briefed me about a case he thought I might be able to help him with. His investigation was at a stalemate at that point and he wanted to bring a witness by for an interview.

We made an appointment for that afternoon, and determinedly optimistic about the outcome, Kevin scheduled a session with one of the department's sketch artists, to follow the hypnotic interview. Actually, I recommended to Kevin that he set up the composite appointment for as soon after Frank Pallermo's session with me as possible. I knew from experience that, if we were to get a description at all from the witness, his recollections would be strongest while he was under hypnosis and immediately after.

Kevin introduced himself and Frank to me amid the noise and hectic activity that reign almost non-stop over the pool of investigators who work outside my office. These men make up the Arson Terrorist Task Force. Like myself, they are under the command of Chief of Detectives James T. Sullivan.

I showed the two men to my office and closed the door, more for privacy than quiet. The sounds of voices and telephones lessened by only a fraction.

As I had done many times before, I started the interview with the aim of putting the subject at ease and allaying any fears and apprehensions about what was going to take place. I asked Frank what his occupation was and what his job entailed. He began to relax a little as he talked. I offered sympathy for the trauma he had experienced and praised him for his generous assistance in the investigation. Then, in more or less the same words I depend on for all first-time subjects, I offered the witness my explanation of the nature of the remarkable mental process he was about to experience.

"Okay, Frank, I know Detective McLaughlin has told you we're going to use a process called hypnosis to help you remember some of the information we're interested in. But it's not the kind of hypnosis you may have seen on television or in the movies. You're not going to become a zombie. You're not going to become unconscious or fall asleep. After all, we want to communicate with you, and if you were unconscious or asleep, we wouldn't be able to do that, would we? So you won't enter a kind of trance state in which you don't have any idea of what's going on. At all times you'll hear everything that's happening. Those fellows in the next room make a lot of noise. You'll hear them talking and yelling out there. You'll hear the telephones ringing and the traffic going back and forth outside.

"If I should happen to bring up something you don't want to talk about, or ask you a question you don't want to answer for some reason, you'll know that I asked that question because you'll always be aware of everything I say and everything you say back to me. If I do ask you something you don't want to answer, you just say to me, 'I don't want to answer that,' or, 'None of your business'—whatever you'd ordinarily do because you'll be in complete control of your faculties at all times. You can even lie if you want to. We can't stop you from lying here. If you like, you can fabricate a wild story about your part in this particular case. What we *can* help you do, however, is recall.

"No one really has an explanation for it, but for some reason, when a person gives in to this relaxed state we call hypnosis, there seems to be an automatic ability to recall. There are a lot of theories as to why this happens. One theory is that most of our memories are stored in what we call the subconscious mind. If we always had to think about everything that happened to us from the time we were born, there'd be so many thoughts buzzing around in our minds that we wouldn't be able to have this conversation. Therefore, we take most of the material we've learned, that we've seen or heard or smelled or touched, and we store it, presumably in the subconscious.

"In this relaxed state we call hypnosis, theoretically your subconscious comes to the forefront. If it's true that our memories are stored there, then it's only natural for these memories to flow out without any strain on your part."

Frank seemed to understand and accept what I was saying and showed signs of being only slightly nervous. I asked him if he had any questions or felt any anxieties about what we were about to do, but his reply was negative. At this point, subjects will often express any of a number of usual fears: "Well, suppose I get into this state and can't get out. What will happen?" This kind of apprehension is almost always based on the false impressions of stage hypnosis—more often than not, the only exposure to the procedure the layman ever has. Because a subject's ability to go into a hypnotic trance depends largely on his capacity to be relaxed and willing, it is important that I seek out and destroy any mistaken notions during the preinduction interview, and assure the witness that there is nothing to fear.

I emphasized that the hypnotic interrogation ahead of us was entirely voluntary, and made sure Frank understood that if he didn't want to do it, we would accept his decision without question. I also told him, "If we're right in the middle of it and for some reason you decide not to continue, you just say to me, 'I've had enough. I don't want to go on,' and we'll stop."

Furthermore, I didn't want Frank to expect something dramatic to happen. "Many of the people who are brought to me to be hypnotized are expecting to be struck by lightning and fall on the floor, or become unconscious and not know what's happening," I explained, perhaps overstating things a bit. "You really won't feel much different than you do right now while we're having this discussion. The most startling thing you may feel is the pleasurable response you get from being at the beach, lying on a blanket with the warm sun shining on you. Your eyes are closed but you're not really asleep because you can hear the kids shouting and playing ball. Maybe somebody calls to you, 'Hey, Frank,' and you hear him but you feel so good you don't want to answer. So he shouts again, 'Frank.' Still you don't want to be disturbed because you feel so comfortable, so relaxed, so at ease. Finally, he says, 'Hey, Frank, what the hell is the matter with you?' And then you grudgingly interrupt your reverie and say, 'All right, what is it?' That's about as dramatic as this thing is going to get, just a nice, relaxed, comfortable, self-assured feeling."

Once a subject is truly convinced that hypnosis is nothing to be afraid of, that while he is under it, I won't betray his trust by delving into private thoughts or past offenses—that even if I did, he would be free to deny them or lie about them—then the subject is in the best possible frame of mind for a hypnotic induction.

Frank gave every indication of being relaxed. He was ready. I switched on the tape recorder, pressed the "record" button, and positioned the microphone for my opening statement: "The date is June 25, 1979, and the time is 1510 hours. This is Sergeant Diggett of the Chief of Detectives Office, and with me is police officer Kevin McLaughlin of the 108th PDU. We're here to interview Mr. Frank Pallermo of 72 Sherman Avenue, Massapequa, New York, about an incident that occurred on Friday, June 22, 1979, at about 1350 hours and carried under case number 626 of the 108th PDU."

The department's lawyers have held fast to the ruling that every hypnotic interview be tape recorded from beginning to end. But legal requirement or not, a permanent record is essential for follow-up by the investigators and for evaluation of my own batting average.

Before beginning the hypnotic induction, I asked Frank to tell me everything he remembered about what took place on the afternoon in question. I pointed the second microphone in his direction, and he described the incident step by step. He added nothing significant to what he had said already in his deposition to Kevin. Nevertheless, this preliminary statement on tape would prove useful in the comparison of Frank's normal-consciousness recollections with those retrieved with the help of hypnosis.

One final preliminary remained. I needed some indication of the degree of Frank's susceptibility to hypnosis in order to choose the most effective method of hypnotizing him. An individual's trance capability is as personal as the way he sleeps, talks, moves. Some subjects respond easily to suggestions of relaxation, while others require a long, involved procedure, and a small percentage can't be hypnotized at all.

To measure susceptibility, I rely on a test called the Hypnotic Induction Profile. Devised by Dr. Herbert Spiegel of the Columbia College of Physicians and Surgeons, and based on extensive research, the HIP is a carefully structured score sheet that assigns numerical values to a subject's responses during a set of prescribed procedures. It begins with what is known as the "eye-roll" method of inducing hypnosis.

To prepare Frank I told him, "I'm going to give you a little test that will give me an idea of how you relax and what might be the best way to help you relax more than you ever have. Are you right-handed?"

"Yes," he replied.

"You don't have contact lenses on, do you?"

"No."

"Good. What I would like you to do now is sit up. That's right, sit back comfortably in the chair, put your feet flat on the floor, and rest your arms on the armrests of the chair like this. In a minute I'm going to ask you to roll your eyeballs up and look into the top of your head, which isn't easy to do, but give it a try. While you're doing it, don't tilt your head up but keep it level like this."

I demonstrated the maneuver.

"Just roll your eyes up as though you had a little bird perched on your head and you're trying to look at it. While you keep your eyes looking up, slowly close your eyelids. When you start to close the lids, they may flutter a bit, but don't let that bother you, okay?

"Now keep your head straight and roll your eyes up. Go ahead. That's the way. Keep looking up and slowly close your eyes, slowly, slowly. Now take a deep breath . . . exhale . . . let your eyes roll back down to their normal position, but keep them closed and let your body float. Just imagine that your body is floating, floating, right down through the chair. You'll find something very welcome, very pleasant, about this sensation of floating."

Frank had no trouble rolling his eyeballs up and keeping them up while bringing his eyelids down. This was a good beginning. After research with thousands of subjects, Dr. Spiegel concluded that anyone who isn't able to separate eye from eyelid movements in this way cannot be hypnotized, except perhaps with great difficulty.

I went ahead with the next test in the induction profile.

"As you concentrate on your body floating, I'm going to con-

centrate on your left hand and left arm. In a few moments, I'll
stroke the middle finger of your left hand. When I do, you'll
develop little sensations of movement in that finger. These sensations will grow, and then a feeling of lightness and buoyancy
will come over your left hand and arm. And you'll just let your
left arm float up into the air as though it were a lighter-than-air
balloon.

"First on the finger, just like that—a feeling of lightness and
buoyancy—and you just let your arm begin to float up as though
it were free of gravity, just sort of floating in the breeze."

Frank's arm rose slowly into the air.

"Just keep it going. Keep lifting it higher and higher, all the
way. Try to feel the contradictory sensation of your body floating one way and your arm floating the other way. Good."

Frank's arm was extended straight out in front of him. He was
responding well and already showing promise of being an excellent subject. I was relieved and, I might add, getting more
relaxed myself.

"There you go. Just let it rest like that. You'll allow your arm
to remain in this position even after I give the signal for your
eyes to open. As a matter of fact, after your eyes are open, if I
should put your hand back down on the arm of the chair, it will
begin to float right back up to where it is now. And you'll find
something very amusing about that situation. Later, when I
touch your left elbow, normal sensation and control will return to your left hand and arm.

"In the future, if we should want to use this exercise to help
you relax, all I have to do is count from one to three. At one,
you look up, and by the count of three, you allow your eyes to
close, and you just let your body drift and float into a nice, deep,
relaxed state. Every time we do the exercise, it will become
easier and easier and you'll be able to relax more and more
deeply.

"Okay, Frank, now I'm going to reverse the process. I'll count
back from three to one, and I want you to follow along with me.
Three, get ready. Two, with your eyes still closed, roll up your
eyeballs. Do that now. And one, slowly let your eyes open."

Frank opened his eyes, blinked a few times, and took a deep,
relaxed breath.

"Stay in that position with your arm raised and tell me how you feel. Are you comfortable?"

"Yeah."

"Do you have any little tingling sensations . . . anywhere in your fingers?"

"No."

"Anywhere else—in your feet, thighs, back of your hands, face, chest?"

"No, nothing."

"Do you feel as though your left hand is not quite as much a part of your body as your right hand?"

"Yeah."

"Now note this." I put his left hand down and it floated right back up.

"How about that? Surprise you?"

"Yes."

"If you saw that happening to someone else, would you believe it?"

"No, I wouldn't."

"As a matter of comparison, pick up your right hand. Do you feel as though you have more control over one hand than the other?"

"Yes, I do."

"Which hand?"

"The right one."

"In other words, if you put this hand down here now and just sort of laid it there, is it going to stay there?"

I put Frank's left hand down on the armrest, but it had a life of its own and immediately floated back up. I answered my own question:

"No, it's going to come up again, huh? Isn't that amazing?"

Frank smiled and shook his head in disbelief.

"Okay, I gave you a signal before that would stop this from happening. The signal was . . . maybe you remember . . . 'Later when I touch your left elbow, normal sensation and control will return to your left hand and arm.' Do you remember me saying that?"

"Yeah, I remember that."

"I'm going to touch your left elbow like this. Now do you have the same control in each hand?"

"Yes."

Frank had accepted the post-hypnotic suggestion. He was responding beautifully. I wondered if he had experienced the sensation of floating, another indication of his level of suggestibility.

"You're doing great, Frank. Since the time we started, when I said to you, 'Just let your eyes close and let your body float,' did you have any floating sensations?"

"Yes, light floating sensations."

"Okay, very good. You have a good score on the profile, Frank. The highest you can get is a five, but this happens so rarely that we don't count it. So four is about the best, and you have three, which puts you very high on the scale of being able to let yourself get into this nice, relaxed state. This is good because it'll save us a lot of time.

"What we're going to do now is virtually the same thing. We'll use the eye-roll technique to help you relax, and I'll give you some suggestions about being peaceful, tranquil, restful, to try to get you even more relaxed than you were a few minutes ago. Then we'll go back to the scene of the crime and see if we can help you remember more. By the way, you were in this state we call hypnosis just a while ago. I'm sure you didn't feel that much different, did you?"

"No, I didn't feel any different."

"And if I said to you, 'When I count to three, you're going to jump out the window,' would you have done that?"

"No."

"But I know you were under hypnosis because you followed what we call a post-hypnotic suggestion. I told you while you were under that after I brought you out of hypnosis, your arm would float right back up when I put it down onto the arm of the chair. Ordinarily it wouldn't do that, would it?"

"No, it wouldn't."

"All you have to do, now that you're an expert, is just look at me and we'll do that same thing."

I put Frank under again with the eye-roll induction, and started working at getting him into a deeper state, returning to the imagery of floating.

"When doing this, some people like to imagine that their body is floating up. Others imagine that their body is floating away on a big, white, cottony cloud. Still others like to think that they're sinking down into a nice, warm, soft waterbed. Whatever image will help you flow into a dreamy, drowsy, comfortable state, that's what you should concentrate on now.

"Feel your muscles relax. Feel your mind relax, getting quieter and more peaceful, more at ease. Your body is slowing down. Your mind is slowing down. Even time seems to be slowing down. There's lots and lots of time, and you feel more at ease, more at peace with the universe, at peace with yourself. So peaceful . . . so quiet . . . so relaxed . . . so tranquil and so calm. As you breathe easily and gently, you feel yourself relaxing more and more with every breath."

I continued in this necessarily repetitive fashion, with slow, almost whispered incantations of calm, peace, tranquility. Frank's body grew steadily more limp as it freed itself of its last vestiges of tension and stiffness. His head began to droop slightly and his breathing became slower and deeper.

"Just let go," I encouraged him. "It feels so good. Leave all your cares, all your worries, far behind and allow yourself to float and drift. Even though you're relaxing more and more, you can still hear my voice clearly and distinctly. You're also aware of the sounds of everyday living that we spoke about before—people talking, perhaps telephones ringing, and traffic going by. But you don't have to pay any attention to those extraneous sounds, unless you have some special reason to. All you have to do is listen to the sound of my voice, which is pleasing to your ears, and keep relaxing more and more with every word I say."

Frank was now in a good, solid trance. But to be sure I had plumbed the depths of his hypnotic capacity before beginning the interrogation, I decided to use a standard deepening procedure. I told Frank that now I was going to count from ten down to one, with the word "deeper" between each count. I asked him to count along with me silently, and suggested he would feel more relaxed with each decreasing number.

At the end of the deepening process, I assured Frank, "You'll be able to stay in this deep, relaxed, comfortable state with your eyes closed until I ask you to open them. Nothing will really bother you. Nothing will disturb you. You just keep breathing deeply and regularly and keep relaxing more and more.

"In a few moments I'm going to ask you to allow your mind to drift and float back through time, back through space, back to Friday, June 22, a day you'll never forget, a day when something happened. The events of that occasion are stored safely in your memory banks. And when I ask you to allow your mind to drift back to that day, you'll be able to let those memories flow out easily and effortlessly. You'll be able to see the events of that day happening all over again. And you'll remain in a deep, calm, relaxed state while you describe to me everything that happened. You'll find you can speak easily and still remain in this relaxed state, almost like a person who talks in his sleep. As a matter of fact, the sound of your own voice will seem to have a special quality that keeps relaxing you. In other words, every word you say will send you deeper into hypnosis.

"When you describe the scene, the actions of that day, I'd like you to speak in the present tense, as though it were happening right now. Instead of saying to me, 'I looked up and saw a man standing there,' you'll describe it in this manner: 'I look up and I see a man standing there.' Sticking to the present tense will help make your recollections more vivid.

"Time and space have no meaning in hypnosis. They just don't seem to matter. We can put ourselves anywhere we want to. So allow your mind to go back now, back, back, back to June 22. You're having lunch in the warehouse with Ralph Kovacs. It's about one-fifty in the afternoon. Tell me what you're eating."

Frank was so relaxed at this point that his voice took on a deep monotone and his speech was drawn out and slightly slurred.

"I had a Muenster cheese sandwich on a hero with a can of Coke."

"I want you to talk in the present now, Frank."

"I have . . ."

"See yourself eating. Are you sitting down or standing up?"

"I was sitting and then I stood up."

"Okay, see yourself standing up. Do you have this sandwich . . . what did you call it?"

"Yeah, a Muenster cheese sandwich."

"Where are you standing?"

"We were in the rear of the warehouse where we do most of our telephone work and prepare our orders. I was standing behind the counter. I was on one side and Ralph was on the opposite side."

"I want you to talk to me as if it were happening right now. I am standing . . ."

"I am standing on one side and Ralph was on the other."

"Ralph *is* on . . ."

"Is standing on the opposite side of the counter."

"Thatta boy, Frank. Now see yourself there, standing on one side and Ralph on the other. Does he have a sandwich also?"

"No, he isn't eating a sandwich. He went out to eat."

"What's he doing?"

"He just finished making a phone call to the office."

"What happens now?"

"A man with a gun, with a ski mask on, comes through the door."

"And what happens?"

"He just keeps pointing the gun, at Ralph, at myself."

"Are you afraid when he does this?"

"We were both stunned at the time."

"Does anybody say anything?"

"Yeah, Ralph said, 'What is this, a joke? What kind of joke is this?' Like I said, Ralph was going toward him and then I heard a shot fired. Once the shot was fired, the guy backed out the way he came in."

Frank's story was unfolding pretty much as it had when he told it without benefit of hypnosis. There were few changes and nothing of consequence was added. When we got to the moment when he was grappling with the perpetrator, I asked him, "Now while you're fighting, there comes a time when you get the mask off a certain amount, right?"

"Yeah, partially . . . you know, not completely off."

"See that happening in your mind's eye. See that mask off as much as it can possibly be and then sort of stop the action as though it were frozen on a screen . . . like instant replay during a football game on television. See yourself looking at that face, as much as you can see of it, and describe it to me."

"I didn't see anything as far as any scars or . . ."

"How is his hair?"

"It was short. He didn't have, like, an Afro or anything."

Frank didn't seem to want to speak in the present tense. I gave up trying, so as not to disrupt the nice trance state we had.

"Does he have sideburns?"

"I didn't notice any sideburns."

"Can you see his eyes and his nose?"

"His eyes? I really didn't get a close look at his eyes. His nose was flat. It was pushed in."

"Is he black or white?"

"He was more like a black person."

"What else?"

"I didn't see a mustache. There was no beard."

"How about his lips?"

"His lips? They weren't really that big or anything—normal I would say."

"Average lips?"

"Yes, average."

"His teeth?"

"I didn't really . . . I really didn't see his teeth. As far as that . . ."

"Have you ever seen this person before?"

"No, I've never seen him before."

"Have you ever seen him since?"

"No."

"If you see him again, will you recognize him?"

"I think I would."

"If I were an artist, could you tell me enough about him so I could make some sort of picture, a drawing?"

"Yeah, I think I could."

We went over the struggle once more, and I asked Frank what he did when he was shot.

"I was conscious all the time. Then after the gunshot, the guy just ran out. He pulled the mask back down and ran up the street. He kept looking back while he was running."

"Where are you now?"

"I was standing at the doorway. I didn't go out of the building."

"Okay, watch him running. Keep seeing him running. . . . Do you see anybody else on the street?"

"I saw people to the left. There's a bus stop on the corner and a diner."

"Do you know any of the people who are there?"

"No, I wouldn't know any of those people."

"Do they see this fellow running out?"

"I imagine they did see him, but like I say, they were either coming out of the diner or possibly going to eat in the diner, or waiting. . . ."

"Is there anybody you know on the street?"

"No, nobody I know."

"What do you do now?"

Frank told about closing the door, calling the main office and John Terry phoning for an ambulance. There was nothing here we hadn't heard before. I decided to try a little technique that had been successful in retrieving more information from witnesses in other cases.

"Just relax now, Frank. Take a deep breath and make yourself comfortable. Let yourself go. Let yourself become more tranquil, more relaxed. I'm going to count from ten to one. While I'm counting, I want you to see this thing again. While you're going over the scene, some little fact you haven't told us about the perpetrator will pop into your mind. Something you haven't thought of will suddenly occur to you. It may be something you saw, something you heard. It could even be something you felt. While I'm counting, if anything pops into your mind, you just start to talk about it. You don't have to wait for me to finish the count. Just see this happening all over again, okay?"

I counted very slowly and watched Frank for some sign of enlightenment. I finished the count without stopping and waited a minute or so for Frank to say something. But nothing came to him, so I spoke.

"I want you to think about the gun for a minute. Which hand does he have the gun in?"

"He had both hands together on the gun."

Until now, Frank consistently had said that the suspect held the gun with one hand. We were making progress. I forged ahead.

"Look at his hands on the gun. Does he have any jewelry on?"

"At the time, I didn't notice if he had any jewelry on his hands."

"Never mind, 'at the time.' Try to see it in your mind's eye now, as you remember it. Try to see him pointing that gun."

"I don't remember seeing . . . I didn't see any jewelry."

"Can you tell me about his shoes?"

"I really didn't get a look at his shoes."

"But as you see him running across the street, you do see the shoes, right?"

"Yeah, I saw him running but I didn't take note of his shoes."

"Can you notice them now?"

"I really can't. . . . I don't recall the shoes."

"Okay, Frank, I'd like to ask Officer McLaughlin if he has any questions he wants to ask you at this time."

"Yes," Kevin jumped in immediately. "When the perp said, 'Lay on the floor,' did he have an accent?"

"I really didn't hear an accent."

Then I asked, "When you're wrestling with him, do you smell anything—shaving lotion or anything at all?"

"No, I didn't smell shaving lotion . . . if anything, more like wine."

That one made Kevin's ears perk up. He said, "You smelled wine?"

Frank responded with a strong affirmative.

I could see the wheels turning in Kevin's mind. He seemed to regard this fact as significant. After mulling over the new information for a moment, he asked, "Recall now, was the smell of wine on his breath?"

"Yeah, it was pretty strong."

Kevin thought about this for a second before saying, "Do you remember seeing a pair of glasses fall on the floor?"

"No, I don't."

"Do you remember seeing a watch when you were wrestling with this guy?"

"No. After he left, I was looking for *my* watch. I didn't see it on my wrist, and then I saw one lying on the floor. When I picked it up . . . It wasn't mine and I just put it back down."

"When you saw him run outside," Kevin continued, "did you see any trucks out there, unloading or parked?"

"No, I didn't see any trucks."

"Did you see a bus go by?"

"No, the street was clear when he ran across it."

"How many people were at the bus stop?"

"Well, it wasn't even at the bus stop. It was past there. It was, like, a little construction outfit after the diner. People were just standing on the sidewalk."

"Were they all men?"

"There were men and women."

"Is there anybody on the construction site?"

"No, nobody was there. It's just a yard where they keep construction equipment."

Kevin had no further questions. Almost an hour had gone by since Frank's induction. It was time to bring him back to normal consciousness, but not without offering a final explanation, this one having to do with a curious post-hypnotic phenomenon.

"Frank, you've done a great job and we appreciate it. I just want to explain something that happens sometimes when we have an interview like this. We seem to get the thought processes stirred up, and later on—an hour from now, two hours from now, in a dream tonight, or maybe even tomorrow—something you haven't told us about this case may suddenly pop into your mind. It could be anything. If it does, please write it down because it'll also have a tendency to pop out of your mind. The smallest detail may be very important, and we wouldn't want you to forget it. So if anything at all occurs to you, just write it down, and give Detective McLaughlin a call.

"Now in a few moments, I'm going to count from one to five. On the count of five, I want you to open your eyes. When you do, your mind will be clear and alert. You'll be refreshed, relaxed, and rested, and you'll feel perfect in every way. When I say five, you'll feel better than you have in a long, long time. And you'll remember everything that you said and we said here today, okay?

"One, you're starting to emerge now . . . two, you're coming up feeling fine . . . three, waking up . . . four, your eyes are opening . . . and five, you're wide, wide awake."

Frank sat up straight in the chair and took a deep breath. He looked as though he had had a good time.

"How was that, relaxing?" I asked.

"Yeah, it was."

"Good. Were you able to see some of those things again in your mind's eye while we were talking about them?"

"Yes."

"Fine. As I said, something else may pop into your head a little later today or some time in the future. If it does, make sure you write it down and don't forget it, okay?"

As Frank assured me with a nod, I made one last comment for posterity before turning off the recorder: "The time is now 1602 and this is the end of the interview."

Kevin was surprised and happy at the results of the hypnotic interrogation. He and I were both amazed that Frank was able to remember a face that he had seen for just seconds and in the middle of a struggle for his life. Kevin had heard his witness say things about the suspect's facial characteristics that no amount of professional strategy or cajolery was able to elicit from him before. He rushed Frank down to the waiting police artist, and a composite of the alleged killer's face was drawn.

The detective had discovered a new and valuable forensic tool, cause for any investigator to celebrate. His enthusiasm came through loud and clear over the phone the next day: "The witness always said he thought he could remember this guy's face, but under hypnosis, he got a more vivid picture. I can remember faces, but to have somebody draw it from your description is another thing. Frank gave me a great composite. He had an intense impression of the suspect because he had actually relived the incident just minutes before. I mean, it must be like watching a ball game on TV and seeing an instant replay. You might've thought you saw a particular tackle clearly, but when it's run by you again, you see it differently. It's isolated and slowed down."

Always in search of a better way to explain how hypnosis heightens memory, I was impressed by Kevin's excellent analogy.

Although Frank had none of the spontaneous flashbacks that sometimes follow a hypnotic interview, the session had provided Kevin with some new leads. He had a composite to show to witnesses of related factory and warehouse crimes; he learned that the suspect had held the gun with two hands, in the style of the police and the military, and that his breath had reeked of wine.

To the untrained, the odor of alcohol might seem insignificant, but Kevin knew otherwise. He was aware that drug addicts in a methadone rehabilitation program often like to drink wine after their treatments. This gives them a super high, almost as if they were on junk again. So the investigator took the composite to a drug center in his precinct and to others in the immediate area. He also visited some liquor stores, but didn't have any luck with either.

He backtracked every related incident, some fifty in all. He didn't find a single witness or victim who would make a positive identification from the sketch. Kevin told me, "Everybody knew I was working on a homicide, rather than a simple robbery or assault, so they tended to lean away from me. They didn't want to get involved. Some would look at the picture and say, 'No, that's not him.' Others would hardly look at it. One witness even said, 'Yeah, that looks like him. The nose is right, the mouth is right, the face is right, but I'm not sure it's him.' I was running up against a lot of fear. But one of the employees at the Harrison warehouse did say that the drawing resembled a guy who had come in looking for a job about three weeks prior to the shooting."

Then it happened again. About a month after the Kovacs killing, a gas station on Twenty-first Street was robbed—same ski mask, same small, silver revolver. Though the victim, the owner of the station, never got a look at the perpetrator's face, he said, "That's the guy who robbed me last year," when Kevin showed him the composite.

In this case, the detective had the good fortune to find two young women who had seen the suspect leaving the scene with his mask off. They reported that he kept looking back at the station, but wasn't running and seemed to be "the calmest person in the world." He even said hello to the women. They told Kevin that they thought the fellow was someone they had seen at Woodside Housing, a Queens apartment complex.

"I canvassed Woodside Housing," Kevin recalled, "and came up with a liquor store proprietor who told me the composite looked exactly like one of his regular customers. I asked the owner to call me if this guy came in again, and to get his name if he could. Months passed and I never heard from him. Meanwhile, the robberies were still going on—about one or two a month. I kept showing witnesses the composite, and if they saw the suspect's face at all, they kept giving me this business about his looking like Muhammad Ali, and no more."

Kevin's break in the ski mask capers came when the owner of the liquor store dropped a dime. He called to say he had just cashed a check for the man in question.

Kevin now had a name. He put a search through the BCI computers and came up with the fact that this man had a record for a previous robbery. He got hold of a picture and was amazed at how much the person in it resembled the sketch drawn from Frank's description. Kevin tucked the shot among twenty-four others and showed them all to Frank. The witness/victim had no trouble picking out his assailant. "That's the guy, that's him," he said without a trace of doubt.

The killer was taken by surprise in his own apartment. He made a dash for that handy little revolver of his, but stopped dead in his tracks. He knew he didn't stand a chance against half a dozen officers with drawn guns. The guy screamed and carried on like a trapped animal, vehemently denying any knowledge of the homicide or robberies. But when he was told he was under arrest, he offered no resistance.

Kevin's star witness was brought in to pick out the perpetrator in a lineup. Unfortunately, the man was too afraid of retribution to go on record as fingering a killer. He told Kevin that, even though he recognized his attacker among the men in the lineup, he couldn't bring himself to point him out. In the absence of any other concrete evidence, the alleged killer was set free.

Such are the ironies of professional investigation—months of hard work ending in frustration. But intrepid Kevin McLaughlin had uncovered an ex-con with a bad case of criminal recidivism. He intended to keep tabs on him, while continuing to try to get a positive identification from any of the few victims who had seen him unmasked.

Kevin called a few days after the arrest and thanked me for

my help. "Hypnosis gave me the lead that tied things up," he said. "Without going to that liquor store and without a good composite, I wouldn't have gotten close to him."

About six months later, I met the detective at a training session, and he remarked, "It was a damn shame we didn't get an arraignment in that warehouse homicide. But you know something, Charlie, there hasn't been a single incident fitting that MO since last September when we arrested the guy."

3

A PHENOMENON ACCEPTED

Despite the dead end of the warehouse homicide investigation, I couldn't help feeling pleased about my own contribution. I was proud that hypnosis had reaffirmed its value as a forensic tool, and I was charged with a sense of real accomplishment, the one sure thing that will make any job personally fulfilling.

It is hard to believe I have been doing this work now for five years. It seems like only yesterday that I got the go-ahead that turned me into the New York City police's first official hypnotist. November of 1976 actually marked the start of the program that would eventually use my hypnotic abilities in over four hundred cases. These include just about all of the city's nationally publicized investigations—the Son of Sam homicides, the Renee Katz subway assault, the Metropolitan Opera homicide among them.

I can't imagine anyone enjoying his job more than I do. To

me, there isn't another slot in the department that comes close to being as interesting. Every day is an adventure. I never know when I get to headquarters what bizarre new case I will be called in on, or what further challenge lies in wait for hypnosis. And I work steady nine-to-five tours of duty with most weekends off, a kind of normalcy unheard of in my profession. But this civil servant's dream job and the acceptance forensic hypnosis enjoys in New York today are not so much the just rewards of hard work. They are more the spoils of a dark horse victory against overwhelming odds.

If there is one thing I have learned in my twenty-nine years as one of New York's finest, it is patience. The wheels of government bureaucracy turn slowly, if at all, and the law-enforcement agency of a giant metropolis is no exception. I was patient during the slow but steady climb up the ladder to the rank of detective sergeant. I was patient in dealing with the constant frustrations of the criminal justice system. And I mustered more patience than I thought I could when my ideas for improvements in the internal operations of the department fell on deaf ears.

A suggestion that finally made the grade was the establishment of a unit in investigative hypnosis. For years I figured that my hypnosis hobby and my law-enforcement career were the most unlikely bedfellows. But it was the happy marrying of the two that gave me a peach of a new command and the Big Apple its first taste of forensic hypnosis.

This is not, however, a story of overnight success. In fact, I would have to go back some time for a complete picture of how it all happened.

I was born in Central Falls, Rhode Island, on August 18, 1927. I was still in diapers and not yet walking when my parents moved me to New York. We settled in Gerritsen Beach, a small seaside community sandwiched between Sheepshead Bay and Floyd Bennett Field in Brooklyn. In summer, the ocean dominated life in Gerritsen Beach. Anyone in town worth his salt could swim, and I earned my own water wings at an early age. Winters were filled with school, P.S. 194 and James Madison High. My father drove a horse and wagon for Borden Milk. He hadn't had the job very long when he fell under the wagon and broke a leg. The break mended but he was no longer able to hop on and off the wagon easily. So he left Borden and became a painter and wallpaperer, a calling he followed off and on for the rest of his working life.

When I look back to those days, I realize that the seed of my lifelong fascination with hypnosis probably had already been sown. But it definitely hadn't sprouted. It is impossible for me to put my finger on any single event and say that is what got me started. I do know, at about the age of seven, I had decided that God was a magician.

As a good church-going Catholic, my mother made sure I went to religious instruction every Sunday after nine o'clock Mass. I can remember feeling skeptical about the amazing things I was told there—that God created the earth and the trees and the people. A conversation with my mother when I got home one Sunday stands out in my mind.

"I guess God's a magician," I said. "I don't understand how He can make things appear and disappear. Only magicians do that."

This comment caused my mother to become quite flustered. She hemmed and hawed and barely managed to get out, "There's a big difference between God and a magician!"

That ended the conversation, but I stuck by my innocent belief. By the time I reached the age of ten, or thereabouts, hypnotists were included in the magicians' group. I had seen a movie that showed an impressive individual appearing to be casting a spell over some people. He got them to do ridiculous things and seemed to be in control of their every action. A character in the film called this man a hypnotist. There was only one way I could understand what was going on: A hypnotist had to be a magician. For some time after that, as far as I was concerned, hypnotism and magic were one and the same thing.

As I moved into my early teen-age years, I was hounded—or should I say haunted—by this unshakable curiosity about magicians and the impossible feats they performed. I had to know how the illusions were accomplished and wouldn't rest until I could do them myself. I think I owned every magic set made at the time for fledgling magicians. As each Christmas and birthday rolled around, the answer to the question of what I would like as a present was always the same: a magic set. But what came as a surprise was the disillusionment that set in. The sleights-of-hand revealed by the sets seemed too obvious. The problem, though, wasn't with the tricks. It was with me. As I worked out the mechanics of the illusions, one by one they lost their fascination.

But hypnosis was another matter. To this day, I look at this phenomenon with no less wonder than I did as a child. I am sure part of the reason is that no one in the world has ever been able to tell me how or why it works.

When a magician makes an elephant disappear, people are astonished. But once they are shown how it is done, they say, "Oh, that's easy. It's just a matter of a few mechanical devices." Hypnosis, on the other hand, never reveals itself. Why is a hypnotized subject unable to bend his arm when he is told he won't be able to? Why does memory seem to improve under hypnosis? Why is hypnosis able to numb parts of the body? When the desensitized area is pricked with a pin, the subject feels nothing, though an instrument measuring nerve impulses shows that a pain signal is reaching the brain. How can this be explained? Extensive research has been carried out and there has been much speculation about what goes on in the mind during hypnosis. But when it gets right down to it, no one yet really has the answers.

A gangly kid in Gerritsen Beach didn't have the answers either but he was certainly determined to get them. I was never by a long shot what you might call a studious child. So my weekly trips to the local library were not only a surprise to my parents but to me also. I will always remember with affection the kindly librarian who was only too happy to fan the flames of my curiosity. She steered me in the right direction, and it didn't take me long to devour any and all books having to do with hypnosis. However, this was no great feat because very little had been written on the subject at that time.

Looking back with the wisdom of hindsight, I realize that a lot of what I read then and during the years before I received any formal training contained misleading and downright false information. None of the books I was able to get my hands on, for instance, disputed the mistaken notion—shared by many people today—that a person under hypnosis is powerless to resist the commands of his hypnotist. It took me a long time to understand that a subject in no way gives up his will power. He is free at all times to think and act as he chooses.

Freedom of choice was a luxury few Americans could afford when World War II broke out. Hiring a professional painter and wallpaperer fell with a thud to the bottom of most people's list of priorities. My father had to find a new job. Fortunately for all of us, my uncle Joe was one of the top brass with the Firestone Corporation in New Bedford, Massachusetts. The company was in full production manufacturing machine gun belts and things of that nature for the war effort. Work was there for my father if he wanted it, so he packed us up and we moved to New Bedford.

It was while I was living there that I saw my first live stage hypnotist. I was fifteen and already had been exposed to a few vaudeville-type hypnosis acts in newsreels and on radio. There was no convincing me, though, that these weren't phony. I was sure the subjects were in on the act and the so-called hypnotists were modern-day medicine men, pure and simple.

But Sam Vine was the genuine article. He is a great showman and a Las Vegas headliner today. When I saw him, he was a small-time club performer on the way up. His act left me stunned and a true believer. It included a demonstration that was one of the funniest things I have ever seen. He chose his subjects from the audience and hypnotized them. He gave them all drinking glasses and suggested that when they looked through the glasses, the people in the audience would appear to be naked. Their reactions were hilarious. I knew when I saw the expressions on those subjects' faces and overheard some of their comments later, that I had witnessed the real thing. I was in awe of Sam Vine.

By the time I settled back to earth and the humdrum of day-to-day life, I was annoyed with myself. I couldn't figure out why I hadn't yet been able to do what seemed to be the easiest thing in the world for Vine. I can still feel the flush of embarrassment and anger reddening my face when my rookie attempts failed. Friends and relatives were guinea pigs. They were only too willing to be hypnotized, but when nothing happened, they split their sides laughing. I was anything but amused.

It wasn't until many years later that I realized a hypnotist is only as good as the trance capability of his subject. A showman hypnotist's greatest skill is his ability to pick only the best subjects from among audience volunteers. With the exchange of just a few words, Sam Vine was able to tell right away which people he could rely on to respond well. They are the ones who, at the drop of a hat, would put a lampshade on their heads to get a laugh at a party. They would as soon perform fully conscious the same shenanigans they are asked to do under hypnosis.

In some cases, highly susceptible people don't even need the preliminary of an induction procedure to respond to hypnotic suggestion. As an example of what is known as waking hypnosis, I once saw Harry Arons, an expert hypnotist and teacher, simply walk over to someone he suspected was a good subject and say, "Excuse me, sir, would you mind holding out your hand and making a fist? Now squeeze it tight. When I count to three, you won't be able to open it. One, two, three—try but you can't." And the person wasn't able to open his hand until Harry told him he could. Although there was no attempt to put the man into a trance and he appeared to be fully conscious, he was, to a certain extent, hypnotized as a result of seeing an expert hypnotist in action and concluding that here was someone with a special ability to impose his will on others. All hypnosis is really self-hypnosis and the most responsive subjects are those who can thoroughly convince themselves they are compelled to do what the hypnotist tells them to do.

No such susceptible people came my way at a time when I would have given anything for the smallest taste of success. I now know that my lack of confidence showed so much that people had no trouble picking up on it. They just weren't convinced I was a hypnotist. Besides, I think I was more than a little afraid of succeeding. For one thing, I hadn't the slightest idea of what I would do with someone once I realized he or she was actually in a trance. Would this first subject snap out of it at my command? What would happen if he didn't?

As I looked ahead to my seventeenth birthday, unanswered questions and self-doubts about hypnosis took second billing to a more important matter. A war was on. America was in trouble and I was as patriotic as the next guy. No sooner had I turned seventeen than I joined the Navy—and saw the world, right? No, I was assigned to a destroyer that never left New Bedford except for an occasional maneuver in the mid-Atlantic. The most memorable event of my two-year stint, which ended in '46, was my first score with hypnosis.

I was with a midshipman buddy in our quarters. We were getting ready to go on shore leave and high as kites at the prospect. The guy's name was Hank Schmidt and he had suffered my ramblings about hypnosis once too often.

"Damn it," he said, "if you're such a hot shot, why the hell don't you try it out on me and we'll see what happens."

A curious feeling churned in my stomach. I think my gut was reacting to the sweet smell of possible success. Hank was the kind of guy who wanted to experience everything and I had a hunch he would allow himself to go into a trance.

We sat down on a bunk and I told Hank to relax. I tried out my most practiced induction procedure and, wonder of wonders, he responded. With his eyes closed, his head slowly fell forward and his breathing got deeper. I knew I had made it. At last, I had put someone in a trance. I was really excited. But true to my expectations, I was scared—more scared than I had ever been before.

"What the hell do I do now?" I said to myself.

"Take him out of it," was the only answer that came to mind.

"When I count to three, Hank," I said nervously, "you'll open your eyes and wake right up. One, two, three. Quick, hurry up, Hank, wake up!"

Hank came to as if nothing had happened and I felt a great weight being lifted from me. Within seconds, I was ten feet off the ground. I had succeeded and the subject was okay!

That first induction gave me tremendous confidence, a frame of mind I now recognize as the successful hypnotist's stock in trade. It's the old Catch-22 situation: Success builds confidence and confidence breeds a higher success rate. Today when I sit down with subjects to hypnotize them, I expect them to go into a trance. And they almost always do. I am stymied only by the exceptional few who for some reason don't allow themselves to give in to the experience.

The end of my tour with the Navy brought with it new concerns. However much self-assurance as a hypnotist I had come by, I was faced with re-entering civilian life and finding a way to support myself. My family moved back to New York. I lingered in New Bedford to romance and win the woman of my dreams. Lucille Richard and I were married in 1947 and ever since, Liz, as she is known by those close to her, has shared my life and given me the ammunition I needed in the fight for professional achievement. I wouldn't be where I am without her.

I was nowhere when I came out of the service. So were hundreds of thousands of veterans who were hard at work making a baby boom but who were still without jobs. My first home with Liz was an apartment in a converted barracks at Floyd Bennett Field. This sort of makeshift housing—some no more than Quonset huts with curtained windows—was a familiar sight in the outlying areas of the city during the years following the war. It offered Spartan living, to put it mildly. But like me and Liz, mobs of ex-servicemen and their families were thankful for the shelter, however meager it was.

The pressure to find employment was building. I lacked a college degree or any skills to speak of. True, I had collected a storehouse of knowledge about hypnosis and could boast an ability to hypnotize, but such assets were hardly negotiable on the late 1940's job market. And an instinctive respect for the therapeutic value of hypnosis—to say nothing of my youthful shyness—kept me from even considering a career as a hypnotic showman.

For anyone in my situation at that time, the police and fire departments promised the greatest opportunities. I opted for law enforcement and will always be grateful I did. The decision was one of the best I ever made. No career is without its disappointments and setbacks, but all in all, the department has been really good to me and my family through the years.

I took the New York City police test and passed. The only thing left to do was wait for my number to come up.

In the meantime, I joined a unit of the Air National Guard based right at Floyd Bennett. This was a convenient setup and would keep us in funds until I started working for the department. What I hadn't bargained for was the outbreak of the Korean War. The whole unit was activated and the next thing I knew, I was in California. I think there is a touch of Irish in my ancestry, but it couldn't be enough to account for the kind of luck I have had with the military. Again I saw neither action nor foreign soil. For two years, my job was playing outfield for the Air Force baseball team.

Shortly after I left for California, Liz joined me. The two oldest of our four sons, Dennis and Marc, were born while I was stationed there, and this was a very happy time for us. The place was truly the land of opportunity then. Like others who were part of the westward migration that was swiftly populating the hills and valleys, we were thoroughly taken with the sea air and sunshine and decided we would make the state our permanent home.

Toward the end of my commitment to the Air Force, I went to see the chief of police in San Bernadino about a job. The fast-growing little town required only a medical examination to join its police force. If you passed that and the chief said hire you, you were hired. But Liz's family and mine were firmly settled back east, and we felt we owed it to them and our children to return there. When my baseball-playing tour of duty was up in 1952, we moved to New York.

Having given up the climate of southern California, we were determined, at least, not to forfeit the seaside living we had grown to love. We found a comfortable little place in Rockaway Beach, and I immediately joined the New York Police Department. Because my number had come up the year before, I started out with twelve months of seniority even before donning a uniform.

My modest talent for playing ball, sharpened by a couple of years' practice, inspired the short-lived dream of making it as a professional. But pressing financial responsibilities wouldn't wait for stardom in the major leagues.

After the required six months of training at the Police Academy, my first assignment was as a radio car patrolman for the 101st Precinct in Far Rockaway. I was relieved to discover that my instincts were right; I loved the work. Three years and another son, Eric, later, we moved into a larger house in Bay Shore and ever since, we have remained on Long Island.

Hypnosis never strayed very far from my mind even during this period of new employment and resettlement. But I didn't dare breathe a word about it to my cohorts at work. The discipline wasn't nearly as respectable then as it is now, and the notion that my amateur dabblings were at odds with my image as a staunch protector of the law didn't escape me. I had every reason to fear that the valued respect of fellow patrolmen and chances for advancement by superiors would be jeopardized if the cat were out of the bag. Most policemen, from the men on the beat to the brass at the top of the heap, had about as much regard for hypnosis then as they did for reading tea leaves or gazing into a crystal ball. If I got stuck with the hypnotist label, I knew I would never stop hearing things like, "Hey, Diggett, when're you gonna ask me to look in your eyes?"

On the home front at least, I could give free rein to my alter ego, and rarely passed up an opportunity to practice my craft. As soon as we moved back to New York, Liz took driving lessons to prepare for a test to get a license. She was very conscientious, studied all the rules, practiced a lot, but was extremely nervous about her readiness. I saw a chance to see if hypnosis would be helpful in a situation of this kind.

On the night before the test, Liz was beside herself with anxiety and insecurity. I knew if I could just get her to calm down, she would have no trouble with the examination. I sat her in a chair and told her to relax. I had attempted to hypnotize her on a number of occasions before, but when I would ask her to look into my eyes, she would always get a case of the giggles and I would give up. This time, I tried an induction that involves having the subject gaze at a fixed spot on the wall, and had trouble believing what I was seeing as I watched Liz go under. While I had her hypnotized attention, I said, "You've studied and trained well for your test tomorrow. You realize, when you think about it, you have all the knowledge and ability you need to pass it. The facts are stored in your subconscious and are available to you whenever you want them. Then I gave her a post-hypnotic suggestion: "When you take your test tomorrow, you'll be calm, cool, and collected. Nothing will disturb you."

Liz was fond of the man who had given her lessons, and was invariably relaxed when she was driving with him in the car. This gave me the idea of also suggesting to her that the inspector would seem no different from her instructor, that he would make her feel every bit as comfortable. The strategy worked.

She was completely at ease during the test and passed it with flying colors.

Hypnosis' effectiveness in helping improve test performance has been confirmed to me many times during the years since Liz earned her driver's license. Studying hard and mastering required material only to become helplessly befuddled during an examination is a human failing that seems to respond especially well to hypnotic therapy. Once the anxiety about preparedness is wiped away by suggestions of relaxation and confidence, the battle is at least half won.

Not too many years ago, my oldest son Dennis and his wife Peggy were thinking of relocating to California. Peggy is a dental hygienist and was concerned about finding work there. She decided to fly out ahead of time, take the state's licensing test, and return to New York. That way she would be ready for work as soon as she got to her new home. The prospect made her a bit nervous and the day before she left, she asked me to hypnotize her. While she was under, I gave her a post-hypnotic suggestion that the instruments she would be using during the examination would feel like an extension of her hand.

There was a self-satisfied grin on Peggy's face when she told me, soon after she got back, "My God, those instruments never seemed so easy to use as they did that day of the test." She won her license but never had any need for it. It turned out that she and Dennis changed their minds about moving. They have remained here in the East.

During those years when my children were growing up and I was on patrol, my hypnotic activities continued to be devoted solely to family members and friends. If those close to me asked if I could help them with a problem of some kind, and I thought it might respond to hypnosis, I was only too happy to give it a try. Sometimes it worked and sometimes it didn't but all the time I was learning and my skill was improving. One of the people dear to me who remained doggedly skeptical about my "foolish hobby" was my mother. One day, to my surprise, she swallowed her pride and asked me to hypnotize her. I was sure she was determined to prove to me, once and for all, how much rubbish this hypnotism business was. Despite her negative attitude, she went under and responded to suggestion. I told her she wouldn't be able to bend her arm, and when she couldn't, she was dumbfounded. I would give anything to have a picture of the expression on her face at that moment. Even confronted with this undeniable evidence of hypnosis' effectiveness, though, she refused to give in. To this day, she won't acknowledge the value of my work, but I suspect that deep down, she doesn't quite know what to think.

At social gatherings, my avocation was received with more enthusiasm. It was at dinner parties and the like among new-found friends and neighbors on the Island that my private tinkerings enjoyed their first public displays. Never really comfortable in the role of life of the party, I was always discreet about my hypnotic skill. But if word of it leaked out in conversation, it spread like a ripple through the crowd and there was nothing I could do to stop it. The next thing I would know, there would be one or two people who wouldn't rest until I hypnotized them. I never refused a serious request, but carefully avoided the kind of stage tactics I considered potentially embarrassing and demeaning, and for some people, maybe psychologically harmful.

To suggest to someone, "Now you're walking in the woods and being attacked by a swarm of bees," can be enormously entertaining to an audience but devastating to the subject if he happens to be petrified of bees or allergic to their sting. So I stayed away from that sort of thing and stuck to demonstrations of arm catalepsy (not being able to bend it), of not being able to get out of the chair or remember one's name—suggestions of that nature.

Temporary amnesia has always been a great crowd pleaser. When a subject is persuaded to forget his name or address, people are in awe of the power of the hypnotist. What they don't understand is that the choice is the subject's alone. The hypnotist is merely the medium or the helper. If I say to an individual under hypnosis, "When I count to three, you'll open your eyes, be wide awake, but you won't remember your telephone number until I touch you on the shoulder," he will say to himself subconsciously something to the effect, "Okay, that's all right by me." Then when you ask him his number, he won't remember it, to the amazement of the audience. But if, when you make the suggestion, he says to himself, "No, I'm not going to forget my number," then when I awaken him and ask him, he will tell me his number. And he will look at me a little weirdly, thinking how could I be so foolish to believe he would forget his own telephone number.

If I have a feeling a subject is particularly susceptible, I might say to him, "When I count to three, you'll open your eyes and have no memory of anything that happened since you sat down. You won't even know you were hypnotized." Now he may or may not accept that suggestion, or he may accept part of it. When I awaken him and ask, "Do you remember that you couldn't bend your arm?" he may say yes. Then if I ask, "Do you remember opening your eyes and seeing a picture on the wall where there was none?" he may say, "No, I don't remember that part." He will have selective amnesia. He will decide what he wants to remember, what he wants to forget.

There is very little that is as funny, with no chance of harm, in parlor hypnotism as a subject not being able to get up from his chair. Everyone thinks the hypnotist is exerting a force that the person is powerless to resist. But, although he has accepted the suggestion, if someone in the room yelled, "Fire!" the subject would have no trouble getting out of the chair as fast as his legs could carry him.

When I demonstrate exercises of this kind, I am used to hearing words to the effect, "Well, if you gave me a little more time or if I really tried harder, I'd be able to bend my arm or get out of the chair." But how much time does it take? One second? Two seconds? It is that crucial hesitation that shows the mind has been momentarily persuaded to restrict bodily movement.

In 1963 I had the feeling my upward movement in the department had been restricted too long for comfort. Just as it was beginning to look as though I was destined to be a patrolman in Far Rockaway until retirement, I received notice of a transfer to the Police Academy Firearms Unit. The assignment was to train recruits in the finer points of defensive tactics and the handling of firearms at the department's outdoor range at Rodman's Neck in the Bronx.

Some of the would-be rookies who came to me were so gun shy they couldn't hit the side of a barn at a range of ten feet.

Skittishness about firearms was all that separated them from their sharpshooting peers. On more than one occasion during my four-year tour with this unit, I was sorely tempted to reveal my hidden asset. There was no doubt in my mind that the nervousness of these men and women could be offset by hypnotic suggestion. But too much was at stake at that point for me to venture out of the closet. The trainees had to overcome their handicap by non-hypnotic means, and with time and practice, they did. I had no qualms about borrowing a few confidence-building exercises from the hypnotic repertoire, but managed not to give myself away with a trance-induction procedure. If I had bitten the bullet and gone through the process of hypnotizing the unsteady-handed recruits, I know they could have found their aim faster, and maybe surer. I would still like to see hypnosis applied to training of this kind, not only to eliminate anxiety, but to turn average gunmen into the highest-caliber marksmen.

The stint with Firearms was followed by a return to the 101st. I was there until 1972, the year I went back to the academy to train for the rank of sergeant. I took the required civil service examination and passed. Never again could I be relegated to patrolman status. The future was looking very bright.

My spanking new sergeant stripes earned me a supervisory tour with the 103rd Precinct in Jamaica, Queens. I was in charge of the men and women on patrol and it was no easy job. Being responsible for the welfare of people who are out every day on the front lines was a real challenge, and I value the six months spent at the 103rd as basic training in sustaining the morale of the street forces, the life blood of the department.

With my next assignment, I went from holding officers' hands to whacking their wrists for misconduct. The command may have been new for me but its concerns were still personnel-related. I was put into a slot in the Internal Affairs Division of the First Deputy Commissioner's Office and occupied it for three years. The work entailed the investigation of corruption—bribery, surreptitious operations, and the like—among the ranks. I can say with all honesty that I found it disagreeable, to put it mildly, to have to pin a rap on a fellow officer. Uncovering evidence confirming the suspected wrongdoing of a colleague was a duty I carried out with mixed emotions. On the one hand, I could never condone even the pettiest criminal offense, especially among people pledged to uphold the law. Yet on the other hand, I am all too conscious of the unique plight of policemen everywhere. By and large they are overworked, stressed close to the breaking point, and underpaid. Combine this with constant temptation and almost unlimited opportunity, and you have a situation where you would expect corruption to be the rule rather than the exception.

As great a variety of people as in the world at large can be found in New York's law-enforcement community. All races, nationalities, and strata of society are represented among its thirty thousand members at full strength. It is safe to say that a hefty percentage of these people, especially those with families, was first attracted to the department because of the security it offers. As long as a man does an adequate job and toes the line, he never has to worry about being fired. And he can look forward to a generous pension program, one of the oldest and most comprehensive in the country. Its half-pay retirement promises insurance against an old age of deprivation and, if police employment is begun early enough, the opportunity of a second career later in life. All this is well and good, but when the motivation for becoming a policeman is weighted more toward making a handsome living than protecting citizens' safety—and the dreamed-of riches never materialize—then the temptation to take a bribe becomes almost irresistible.

One of the functions of the Psychological Services Unit is the screening of potential recruits. Tests have been designed to weed out undesirables, those unsuited for police work for one reason or another. In the past, the screening has been effective in keeping most of these people out of the department. But in more recent times, many of those who have been turned down have gone to court to challenge the decision, and the courts have ruled that the department must hire them regardless of the findings of the tests. Ironically, the records show that many of these very people, after becoming police officers, were caught red-handed engaging in criminal activity of some kind.

The judicial system seems to be determined to make the work of law enforcement more and more difficult. The trend in court rulings in favor of the protection of the rights of suspected criminals threatens not only to undermine morale and incite corruption among frustrated police personnel but also to jeopardize the welfare of law-abiding citizens. Any time the court takes a weapon away from law officers, I can't help but feel it is taking something away from society in general. By a weapon taken away, I mean, for example, no longer being able to keep a suspect under surveillance with binoculars or a telescope without getting a court order. Judges reason that if we need the equipment badly enough, we will get the order. They don't realize how much time and effort it takes, and in most investigations, time is crucial. Then there is always the chance, after we have gone through all the red tape, that the order will be denied because we haven't come up with the specific material required for the case in question.

I once heard a Supreme Court judge say, "Why should I make it easy for the police to put people in jail?" I can understand his position, but I can just as easily ask, "Why should he make it impossible for elderly people to come out into the street?" And why should someone known to have committed homicide be allowed to roam free just because of some oversight in his incarceration? There has to be something wrong with a system that permits these things. I think we have the best in the world, but there is plenty of room for improvement.

The city of New York is losing the battle against crime. How can it win when every time it defeats one of its enemies, he's right back out there the next day fighting again? If this situation continues unchecked, it won't be long before New York is a war-torn ghetto uninhabitable by any but the most savage and ruthless. Runaway crime can be stopped only when the populace decides it has had enough, when it takes the stand that people who commit crimes must be removed from society without compromise and that a punishment befitting the offense must be doled out unstintingly. I have great confidence in New Yorkers and am optimistic that they will one day turn the tide.

Toward that end, the department has already taken a step in the right direction with the recent establishment of the Career Criminal Investigation Unit. This specialized task force of twenty-five men focuses on recidivists, those criminals who are arrested on a major-offense charge, serve a nominal amount of time, if any, and are then released, only to be arrested again for the same crime. The unit's game plan is to finger the repeat offender and break the pattern by doing everything it can to put him away for good. Channeling investigative energies in this and other ways holds great promise as compensation for the leniency of the courts.

My head grappled with the dilemmas of criminal justice during the quiet moments that were too few and far between while delving into in-house corruption. I may have been a little slow on the uptake but it eventually occurred to me that if we were to chalk up more victories in the battles against crime, the courts, and personnel frustration, we had to arm our investigators with the best and most sophisticated evidence-scouring weapons science and technology could provide. Did I dare include hypnosis? Yes, the going might be rough but the climate was better than it had ever been since I joined the force. Though not known to the general public at the time, the department had already succumbed to seeking the help of psychics in certain investigations. If it was willing to bet on the existence of extrasensory perception, scientifically unproven and a long shot at best, why not take a chance on hypnosis?

I knew that among the powers of the mysterious-seeming phenomenon was the enhancement of memory. I had seen deeply hypnotized subjects recall random moments of their lives, as far back as early childhood, in minute detail—certainly more vividly than normally possible, even by the most viselike memory. Since most investigations rely on the reports and descriptions given by witnesses and victims, I wondered if hypnosis could help these people, too, remember more of what they saw or heard. Sure enough, I didn't have to wonder for long. At about the time word of the use of forensic hypnosis in other parts of the country began reaching me, I came across a book called *Hypnosis and Criminal Investigation* by Harry Arons. The author outlined a collection of cases in which hypnosis had been applied successfully. Now that I knew others had already been doing what I envisioned, there was no holding me back. I had found the courage to declare myself.

In my impatience to get a New York hypnosis program started as soon as possible, I decided to go right to the top. The

Commissioner of Police in 1974 was Michael Codd. I wrote him a carefully worded letter describing my proposal and citing the precedents. The disappointing response reached my desk a few days later. It was a form letter thanking me for my suggestion and promising to give the matter some thought. I had heard that one before. Too many great ideas had died a quick death in the same way. It would be a gross understatement to say I was discouraged. By not settling for less than the number-one man, I had risked everything and lost.

A year and a half went by without a word from the commissioner's office. I was sure the big boss had decided I was operating with less than a full deck, and had thought about my letter for the last time when he consigned it to his wastebasket. Then a call from the Psychological Services Unit's doctor-detective Harvey Schlossberg caught me off-guard. Somehow the letter had worked its way down to him, no doubt because the commissioner figured that the least he could do was arrange for me to have some psychological counseling, I remember thinking at the time. But no. Harvey was very much interested in my proposal. He wanted me to come by and tell him all about it.

I gave him a complete rundown. Although he was a clinical psychologist, he had had scant exposure to hypnosis. I was so overjoyed at finding someone in the department who was willing to listen to me that I probably overstated the case a bit. But Harvey didn't need much convincing. He is the kind of man no one could ever accuse of being shortsighted, and he had no trouble grasping the potential of boosting interviewees' memories with hypnosis. Besides, he admitted that he had been besieged by calls from both New York and out-of-town investigators who had read the first reports about the new forensic aid. They wanted to know if the department had its own hypnotist who could help them on cases they were having trouble with.

Harvey came up with a scheme. "The next time someone calls," he said mischievously, "I'll say, 'Yes, we have a hypnotist. Come on over.' That'll give us a chance to try it out and see if it works or not."

Our first guinea pig was a teen-age rape victim. The detective who called told Harvey that the young woman couldn't give him any information about the man who molested her, and he had an inkling that hypnosis might be able to cut through the emotional straitjacket the trauma had put her in.

I had my own emotional misgivings to deal with. This would be the first time I would be attempting hypnosis in a forensic situation. I worried about not being able to hypnotize the subject. And if I did succeed, would I uncover anything helpful to the investigation? My convictions were on the line.

I needn't have worried. The young woman went into a medium-to-light hypnotic state and was able to give us a description. And she recalled that her attacker was left-handed, wore a towel around his neck, and had an odor of alcohol on his breath. One curious bit of information also surfaced during the session. The victim somehow managed to hold on to her cat for the duration of the assault—a believe-it-or-not hall-of-fame candidate if ever I heard one.

Although our efforts turned one more investigator into a forensic hypnosis fan, he was never able to bring in a suspect, and the case remains unsolved.

Harvey and I wrestled with nine more cases over the next six months. Out of the total of ten, we turned up new and valuable investigative material in seven—an impressive score for hypnosis. As far as Harvey was concerned, the numbers told the story. "There's no doubt in my mind now that this thing really works," he said. "We've got to get the department to recognize it. Our best plan of attack would be to go after the legal division and press them to give us permission to mount an official pilot program."

I wrote up a five-page memorandum outlining our successes and those of other law-enforcement agencies and asking for no more than the chance for hypnosis to prove itself. The legal experts wasted little time in responding. They refused to give us the go-ahead, justifying their decision with the claim that information gained would be inadmissible in court and that the department would be fair game for people who would sue if they decided the interview had caused them harm. We shot back immediately with a statistic we thought was bound to make them see things our way: Material uncovered by hypnosis had already been admitted as evidence in court in four cases on record. But this had little effect beyond pressuring them to sound forensic hypnosis' death knell with a more determined clang. No way were they going to open the doors of the New York City police to hypnosis, and that was that. Harvey and I were crushed.

If it weren't for a series of events that began right after that, the program would have been beyond rescuing and New York might have remained to this day without an investigative hypnotist. First of all, Chief John Guido, my boss at Internal Affairs, got wind of my hypnotic sleuthing and efforts to gain it official recognition. He called me into his office one day and announced, in no uncertain terms, that if I was going to continue to pursue this hypnosis thing, I had better find myself another job outside Internal Affairs. He explained that it was tough enough to operate there without the cops thinking that every time we called them down for questioning, we were going to pick their brains with hypnosis.

A common misconception had cost me my job. I was getting a reputation as a Svengali who could compel colleagues to drop their guard and reveal their innermost secrets. It was more an amusing development than a disturbing one. I could handle it for a time but was determined to set the record straight someday. I was convinced that a hypnosis education program for all members of the force was the only way I would ever succeed in exploding the myths they clung to.

In a way, I was glad to have an excuse to leave Internal Affairs. I was never crazy about being there to begin with and welcomed the opportunity to look for a command where I could nurture my pet project with impunity.

While trying to find a suitable opening, I heard from Chief Ed Drayer, commanding officer of every detective operating out of Queens. He was interested in the work I was doing and wanted my help on some cases that had fallen under his command. This was really a lucky break. It was the first nibble I had gotten from a high-ranking officer and the first time I felt genuinely hopeful that the program just might get off the ground after all.

Hypnosis got rave reviews in Queens. Chief Drayer was so pleased with the way it expedited his detectives' investigations that he went to bat for me to arrange for a transfer. But when he approached his superior, Chief Cotell, the commander of New York's full complement of detectives, to get clearance to move me, he got a taste of the outrage I had seen time and again in response to the mention of hypnosis. Cotell acted as though Drayer had lost his marbles and practically threw him out of his office. I was back to square one.

But not for long. Good old lady luck came to the rescue again. I heard about an ideal-sounding opening in the Brooklyn detective area and applied for a transfer. It was approved, and before I knew it, I was the commanding officer of the Brooklyn Homicide Task Force. The organization zeroed in on the slippery entanglements of organized crime, and it was my responsibility to keep track of favorite hangouts and shifting alliances, rubouts and vendettas among the ruling families. It was a fascinating tour, though not without the usual frustrations. The honchos of the underworld know every trick in the book to avoid incarceration, and keeping one step ahead of them was a challenge that demanded every ounce of professional expertise I had accumulated up to that point. But without a doubt, the best thing about the tour was my immediate superior, Deputy Chief Anthony Voelker.

Tony Voelker, more than anyone in the department beside myself and Harvey, was responsible for putting hypnosis over the top. He had great faith in its investigative potential, and in him I finally found the influential, high-ranking champion I needed for the top brass to take me seriously. As soon as he found out about the trouble I had run into in getting a program off the ground, he got behind it. The forty-nines (referring to a type of letterhead) bearing his signature started flying left and right, and the brass began paying more attention to what was happening. In the police department, it doesn't matter what your credentials are—Harvey's Ph.D., for example—if you are a detective, you aren't a chief. By and large, as far as the big bosses are concerned, a chief is to be taken seriously, a detective needn't be. This is the way it is. When no one else could, Chief Voelker secured approval for me to take hypnosis courses at a variety of respected institutions and eventually performed the miracle of materializing a go-ahead for an official pilot program.

Another development crucial to the shift in attitude toward investigative hypnosis was a bizarre case that gained nationwide publicity at that point. The July 1976 timing of the kidnapping of a busload of school children in Chowchilla, California, couldn't have been better to further the cause of forensic hypnosis in New York. The abduction had all the elements of high drama, and the nation's attention was riveted to every detail. Twenty-six children and the driver of the bus had been carted away, and their captors demanded ransom. The criminal ingenuity of these men has yet to be equaled. It was quickly discovered that they had buried the whole bus, with its human cargo, beneath the ground, taking great pains to ensure the occupants' survival. As soon as the victims were rescued, they were questioned about their captors, and hypnosis was used to help Ed Ray, the driver of the bus, remember two or three numbers of the license plate on the abductors' car. This led directly to a suspect and the solution of the case. It was clear to the people in America and many other parts of the world that hypnosis had saved the day. It was regarded with new respect, even by the tough-skinned skeptics on New York's police force who were empowered to decide the investigative tool's fate.

The overwhelming impact of this and other cases, combined with the perseverance of Tony Voelker, Harvey, and myself, were too much for the legal division. At last, they reneged and put their seal of approval on a ninety-day pilot program. But they were adamant in demanding that we not deviate from these guidelines: The subject was required to sign four legal releases, the entire procedure had to be tape recorded or videotaped, and under no circumstances were we to hypnotize a suspect or defendant in the case under investigation. The lawyers speculated, with good reason, that the courts would regard the hypnotic interrogation of a suspect as a direct violation of his or her right of due process.

Also, the high-command decision came down tacked with the proviso that each subject had to be interviewed first by a qualified psychologist or psychiatrist, who then had to be present during the hypnotic procedure. The legal eagles of the department insisted on this precautionary measure. But after about a year's worth of cases, it was obvious to everyone concerned that the consultant's presence was superfluous—and, at two hundred dollars a shot, a luxury New York City could ill afford.

There have been no adverse reactions or complications resulting from any of the hypnotic interrogations I have performed, nor, as far as I know, from those conducted throughout the country by other law-enforcement personnel. By an adverse reaction, I am not talking about a little crying and trembling, but a severe hysterical episode in which the subject screams and kicks and otherwise behaves as he might have during the remembered assault. The unwelcome response could be followed, theoretically, by a prolonged period of emotional disturbance. I have never seen, heard of, or read about anything like this resulting from hypnosis. And I have interviewed a number of traumatic rape victims who were under the care of psychiatrists when they were brought to me to be hypnotized. Some of these women agreed to the procedure only if their psychiatrists could be at their sides. This is the way the interviews were done, and, in every case, when the session was over, the attending psychiatrist told me that the hypnosis had benefited his patient, that recalling the incident had relieved some of the trauma.

The fact that psychologists sometimes make use of a technique called abreaction and catharsis is partly responsible, I believe, for their objection to policemen performing hypnosis. The practice is a therapeutic treatment in which the patient is provoked into reliving the disturbing situation at the root of his problem, thereby cleansing his soul, so to speak, and making him feel better. The technique involves true regression, called revivication. The practitioner must be well trained to direct the hysteria the purging may arouse. Psychologists suspect that police hypnotists are going about the same thing without the knowledge it demands. But, in truth, I avoid it at all costs. So do others who have had the same training I have. Unlike the therapists, our aim is far from making the subject relive the incident and stirring up painful emotions. We strive only for the circumstances surrounding a criminal action, recalled as calmly and dispassionately as possible. And this is why we have never come across an emotional situation we couldn't handle.

Our lawyers were concerned that people would sue the department if they found the hypnotic interview to be a severely disturbing experience. The fact that, after more than four hundred interviews, we haven't had a single suit, in a city where such legal actions are virtually a way of life, should be proof enough that hypnosis in the hands of policemen is no cause for alarm.

Still, some professionals in human behavior insist that a police officer trained in hypnosis is not qualified to practice it. I happen to know personally psychiatrists, psychologists, and physicians who regard themselves as experts in hypnosis. Yet they have received no more training in it than the policemen they would like to see stopped from using it.

An especially outspoken critic of police hypnotists is Dr. Martin Orne, an internationally known expert in the field and the editor of a psychology periodical. Dr. Orne claims that police officers are inclined to accept the information secured through hypnosis as fact, and are unaware of a hypnotized person's capacity to confabulate or of his eagerness, in his suggestibility, to tell the officer what he wants to hear.

The truth is that professional investigators are experts in the art of interrogation. Nearly every day, they find themselves up against witnesses fantasizing and victims too willing to please or accuse. They learn to sniff out the credible from the useless. It is part of the job. And those trained to hypnotize expect the same from a witness in a trance. These officers know that subjects can lie, fantasize, misinterpret, or even refuse to answer as easily as they can when fully conscious.

What Dr. Orne seldom emphasizes is that investigative hypnosis is just another tool—like fingerprinting, ballistics, composites —to help the investigator gather information. He needs an arsenal of bits and pieces to weave the fabric of a conclusive case, and many evidence-retrieval techniques have been developed to serve that end. One of the newest now being put to the test is role playing. Witnesses or victims are asked to act out, rather than describe, the circumstances of the crime. So far, this strategy is proving effective in helping people remember events more accurately.

In their quests for the truth, investigators will use as many of the lawful means at their disposal as they can. But whatever the source of a piece of information, it must be corroborated by other evidence. I am always careful to point out to the officers at my seminars that statements made by an interviewee under hypnosis have got to be checked out. It has been my experience, though, that these men and women hardly need to be told that. No trained investigator is going to base a case on evidence uncovered solely by hypnotic interrogation. And neither will the courts convict a defendant on that basis. Recent trials indicate this very clearly.

The point is that forensic hypnosis is useful so long as it remains a single component among the many that make up a total investigation. A hypnotic interview can shed new light on a case or prod an investigator to consider another avenue of pursuit, but the evidence it reveals should never be regarded as conclusive.

Though some members of the psychological and medical establishment would have people believe otherwise, every expert therapist or physician isn't necessarily knowledgeable about hypnosis, especially the forensic variety. On a number of occasions, I have watched trained psychologists bungling the hypnotic interviews of witnesses or victims. By and large, the hypnosis techniques of these professionals couldn't be faulted. But their work was useless from a forensic point of view because they kept asking leading questions inadvertently. They put words in their subjects' mouths and led them to hasty conclusions without even realizing what they were doing. The subjects picked up on all sorts of aural and—if their eyes were open—visual cues. It doesn't take much—an inflection of the voice, a widening of the eyes, or a barely detectable smile. The psychologists showed their ignorance of the pitfalls of interrogation. They had none of the technique that is the stock in trade of any experienced investigator.

I don't mean to imply that the two backgrounds couldn't be combined to make one neat professional package. In fact, where hypnosis is concerned, this is probably the ideal. Men and women with in-depth training in both psychology and law enforcement aren't unheard of in today's police-agency network. Harvey Schlossberg, who has a doctorate in psychology and is the author of *Psychologist with a Gun*, served in the past as Director of our Psychological Services Unit. At the same time, he was a detective, a sworn member of the department with all the training and experience of an officer of his rank. As a policeman, he was better equipped than a civilian psychologist would have been to handle the professional problems of the men he counseled. I don't think he could have served the department as brilliantly as he did if he hadn't been one of its full-fledged members.

On the other hand, Dr. Martin Reiser, the psychologist who heads our psych services counterpart in Los Angeles, hasn't signed the book, as we say, or taken the oath; he isn't a sworn member of the L.A. police, but he has had years of experience in law enforcement and is a forensic hypnosis pioneer. He established L.A.'s hypnosis program and it is still going strong. When I went out there to observe his operations in 1976, he had eighteen trained hypnotists working under him. These men and women were all law officers, however, who performed hypnotic interrogations in addition to their other, more routine investigative duties. Whoever was available when a hypnotist was needed would be called on to conduct the interview. I happen to like our system better. I think it makes more sense for the hypnotist to be free of all other work. His energics won't be dissipated nor his objectivity tainted if he is not held responsible for clearance rates, number of arrests, and other bureaucratic paper shuffling.

Implied in the psychological community's criticism of police hypnotists is that, as law-enforcement personnel, we lean toward the conviction side of a case, that we have an ax to grind and are out to nail a particular person. But this just isn't so. A professional investigator takes great pride in his impartiality. As far as my own situation is concerned, my involvement in the investigations is purely as a consultant. It makes no difference to me what direction a case takes or who is or isn't implicated. I make a point of getting as little information as possible from the detectives in charge. This minimizes the risk of leading questions and makes my work more effective.

The hypnotic interviews I like best are those where information nobody could have foreseen comes out spontaneously. In a number of instances, the people connected with a particular case hadn't the slightest idea what the suspect looked like, for example, or what the model or color of the car was. And these things popped out under hypnosis and were then corroborated. In one case I am especially fond of, it turned out that there wasn't even a crime involved.

A man was washing his car in the street in front of his house. His eight-year-old son was playing ball on the lawn with a neighbor's nine-year-old daughter. The man suddenly heard a thud and turned to see his son lying in the middle of the street and a car driving away. Fortunately, the boy wasn't severely injured. He was banged up a bit and one leg was broken.

The detective assigned to the hit-and-run brought the father to my office. The only thing the man remembered about the car was that it had a two-tone paint job. The investigator was counting on the hypnotic interview to help his witness come up with the year and model, and maybe even the license number.

Under hypnosis, the man remembered that the car was a two-door Cadillac and that it was occupied by an elderly man and woman, both with gray hair and glasses. He also recalled seeing a New York registered plate, but the numbers on it were beyond his recollection.

When the interview was over, the investigator and I were discussing the case and the witness was off by himself smoking a cigarette. He was pensive, staring into space.

All of a sudden he said, "She pushed him."

I turned toward him and said, "Who pushed who?"

"The little girl who was playing with my son. She pushed him. They were playing ball and the ball rolled away. The kids ran after it. My son was there first, picked up the ball, started to run, and the girl pushed him right into the side of the car."

The whole incident came back to him in a flash of hypnotic perseveration. This is the word—related to persevere—hypnotists use to describe the lingering suggestibility and heightened recall subjects experience for a short period after "awakening." In an instant, the memory of what this man had seen was unlocked from his subconscious. Hypnosis somehow broke the code that triggered a playback of the stored images. The children's actions were there for the witness to see, and he was now satisfied the whole thing was an accident. No crime at all had been committed. More than likely, the people in the car drove on completely unaware of what had happened.

Though the father of the victim was convinced of the accuracy of his new-found memory, the detective went after some corroboration. He eventually got it by gently questioning the two children. Interviewed separately, they told the same story: The girl unintentionally had knocked the boy against the passing car. The investigator was convinced. The case was closed.

The hypnotic interview had saved the boy's father untold anguish and the investigator a lot of unnecessary work. And even Dr. Orne would have had to agree that we harbored no preconceived notions about the case. We weren't out to bag a suspect at all costs. Spontaneous recall prompted a disclosure that none of us could have foreseen. It certainly couldn't be said that the witness felt compelled to give us what he thought we wanted.

It is my personal opinion that at the root of the critical bias of the psychological profession is concern more for members' earnings than the well-being of forensic hypnosis subjects. In New York City alone, we have done more than four hundred interviews using hypnosis. This represents a loss of at least eighty thousand dollars to psychologists and psychiatrists—much more if these professionals were to have conducted the hypnotic interrogation, rather than just being in attendance. But when the total in question is multiplied by the hundreds of law-enforcement agencies throughout the country now involved in hypnosis, the size of the revenue loss becomes enormous. As far as I am concerned, the decisive factor here is money, not justice.

It seems to me that there is just no way the social scientists can win this battle. They will no doubt continue arousing unnecessary concern, and may have a few triumphs here and there. But how, in reality, can there be a regulation preventing police officers from hypnotizing anyone? Where does it start? Hypnosis is a natural phenomenon. It sometimes occurs spontaneously. When a witness comes in and the investigator says, "Just sit down here and relax," has he already gone too far? Where is the cutoff point?

Dr. Milton Erickson, a well-known psychiatrist and the number-one medical hypnotist in the country until he passed away recently, was quoted as saying that the medical establishment has considerably exaggerated the dangers of hypnosis over the years in order to maintain control over it. Dr. Erickson firmly believed that there were absolutely *no* dangers in hypnosis.

The only way to convince the psychological community would be to do a follow-up study of thousands of forensic hypnosis interviews. It would demonstrate that no harm whatsoever befell the people involved, that if anything, they felt better afterward than they did before. This would take the therapists' weapon away from them.

The ideal solution to the problem would be the establishment of an institution of some kind specializing in forensic hypnosis training. Both students and teachers would be a mix of police officers, psychologists, laypersons, and doctors. The course of study would represent a meeting of the minds on at least a national level. The standards, practices, and procedures taught would be worked out to the satisfaction of the psychological and law-enforcement communities. It would make me very happy to have a part in the realization one day of this not-too-farfetched dream.

Our ninety-day pilot program, which was launched on November 1, 1976, has never been terminated. The effectiveness of forensic hypnosis was established so conclusively that the transition from pilot program to officially sanctioned investigative unit was an easy one, without any of the authorities ever saying, "Okay, the trial period is over. We can see this thing really works, so let's set it up on a permanent basis."

During that time when I was hypnotizing witnesses and building a case for forensic hypnosis, I was still shouldering the responsibilities of the Homicide Task Force command. I felt like a hamster in a running wheel, and only the hope that hypnosis would be my sole concern one day kept me going. I was grateful for help, and was fortunate to have been offered some in the person of Detective John McGrath.

John has a degree in psychology and, like myself, was a policeman with a special interest in hypnosis. He had been working for Chief Voelker in Brooklyn and, although he hadn't made the inroads Harvey and I had, he, too, was trying to get a hypnosis program going when I arrived on the scene. The chief thought it would be a good idea to team us up, and it was. John and I worked together from the start of the pilot program until January of 1979—more than two years of accomplishment and gaining the confidence of the department's investigators. Although hypnosis had just about won a permanent place for itself on the force, it still had to earn the respect of most of the personnel. An army of detractors would have been happy to see the study fail, but as our successes accumulated, more and more officers began to see the light.

As well as I could, I tried to make my working relationship with John an equal partnership. He hypnotized some subjects and I hypnotized others. Before each session, we talked about the case, and I always asked John what approach he thought we should take. If I felt he had a better idea than I did, we would do it his way. But in the end, rank prevails in the police department. There is just no way of getting around it. Of the two of us, I was the ranking officer and, technically, in command. If we disagreed about something, there was no question but that John would defer to my judgment.

Finally, it was the rank issue that abruptly brought the curtain down on our partnership. Chief Cotell, who was far from being kindly disposed to forensic hypnosis, retired and James T. Sullivan became the new Chief of Detectives. Soon after he had settled into the job, Chief Sullivan contacted me. He disclosed that he was interested in the work I was doing and wanted to bring me over to central headquarters in Manhattan where he could monitor my operations more closely and make them more conveniently available to the entire department. This was unprecedented recognition of the new investigative tool and a euphoric shot in the arm for me. Unfortunately, because of the shortage of manpower, the chief felt he could afford only one investigative hypnotist. Since the choice had to be made on the basis of rank, I was it and John was out of the picture.

It seemed that every step forward demanded some kind of sacrifice in the bargain. I hated losing a valuable associate but could hardly overlook the fact that I had won a long-awaited victory. Chief Sullivan had the good sense to realize that it was in the department's best interests to allow me to stick to hypnosis full time. I was so used to juggling two jobs at once that this new development took a while to sink in. When it did, I was in seventh heaven.

The crisp, impressively modern interior of One Police Plaza didn't quite fit my notion of heaven, but I decided the real thing couldn't have made me feel any better. Working right in the Chief of Detectives Office was like being on top of the world with the chief himself as my guardian angel. He took a personal interest in my work and sat in on some interviews. The more he saw, heard, and learned, the more impressed he was.

One thing that did not impress him, though, was my beard. Shortly after I moved over to his office, he issued a memo to the effect that anyone in the detective division who wasn't engaged in an undercover operation of some kind wasn't permitted to have a beard. A small postscript at the bottom of the memo stated: "Anyone who would like to keep his beard will submit a forty-nine through channels." I was determined to keep mine. It was a neatly trimmed Vandyke and, however unreasonably, it fit my conception—probably dating from boyhood—of what a hypnotist should look like. I submitted a forty-nine to Inspector Rose, my immediate superior and number three in command under the chief, hoping to bring home the point that the beard was essential to my job and morale. He sent it right back with, "I disapprove," in big red letters written across it. So that was the end of the beard. The department, like the military, doesn't tolerate exceptions. In an effort to eliminate the bushy, unkempt beards that some officers were sporting and some citizens found offensive, a blanket order had to be issued and reinforced.

The beard incident was the closest I have come to any friction or unpleasantness between myself and my superiors at the Chief of Detectives Office. Working at central headquarters has truly been like a dream. As more and more investigators seek my help and hypnosis gives them results, everybody is happy. And that includes the press. One thing I never anticipated was becoming a minor celebrity. But I have been inundated with requests for interviews and there is nothing I can do but comply. It is a strange experience seeing my face staring back at me from newspapers and magazines, stranger still to watch myself answering questions on television news and talk shows. But I can't say I don't enjoy it. What I like most about media exposure is the opportunity of contributing to a greater understanding of hypnosis, especially as it applies to police investigation.

One of the happiest moments of my life took place in June 1980. I was given a brand-new, private office and was allowed, for the first time, to put up a sign that read, "Hypnosis Unit." A small headline in one of the New York dailies told the story: "Police Appoint Official Hypnotist." Not until then was it really official. Forensic hypnosis had arrived in New York.

4

A BARRIER BROKEN

Witnesses or victims of brutal crimes are sometimes so overwhelmed by the horror of the experience that they block out all memory of it. The phenomenon, called traumatic amnesia, is described by psychologists as the mind's emergency system for protecting itself against the shock of recalling an especially disturbing incident or situation.

Hypnosis is an amazingly effective tool for breaking through this mental barrier. It seems able to accomplish this without triggering an emotional crisis or, for that matter, any harmful reactions whatsoever. In fact, in my experience, the effect has been therapeutic. The subjects I have helped overcome this form of amnesia appeared relieved once they confronted the painful memory that had been brewing in their subconscious. Every one of them reported feeling liberated from some terrible burden.

In one of the cases involving the phenomenon, a key witness

was able to break through a memory block related to a crime that had occurred eight years prior to the investigation. Hypnosis' power in this instance really astonished me. Not only was the witness able to throw off the blinders of his selective amnesia, he relived eight-year-old events as if they had taken place only days before.

In 1970 in a small town in Rhode Island, Ruth McCormick was reported missing by her second husband, Roy. She was never found. The local police at the time concluded that the incident was a routine disappearance and closed the case.

When Rhode Island law-enforcement jurisdictions were reorganized three years ago, the municipality in which this case took place came under the jurisdiction of the state police. As a formality, the state investigators reviewed a number of old, unsolved cases. They didn't like the looks of this one and decided to reopen it.

By that time, Roy McCormick had moved to Massachusetts with the two youngest of his wife's four children. The two older children had left home, and it was found that the oldest son, twenty-two-year-old Dennis Halper, was serving time in a Georgia prison for a robbery conviction. The Rhode Island police gave Dennis and his stepfather lie detector tests. The young man's statements appeared to be true but there was considerable doubt about his stepfather's.

Dennis told the investigators that all he could remember about his mother's disappearance was that he had been with her at his aunt's house the night before. They drove home together, he went into the house, and his mother drove off. That was the last he saw of her. When there was no sign of his mother the next morning, Dennis asked his stepfather where she was. He replied that she had gone to the next town to look for a job and that she would be back Saturday for her clothes. The boy went straight to his aunt's house. But when the police questioned his aunt, she was certain it was two days later when Dennis actually came to see her.

In addition to this troublesome contradiction, the investigators came across a curious piece of evidence in the case's file. It was a scrap of paper with the words "father kill," written on it, and it had been found in Mrs. McCormick's car. Dennis remembered nothing about it.

The state police decided to try hypnosis. They were hopeful that it might enable Dennis to remember whether or not he had written the note, or bring some other long-forgotten detail to the surface—anything that would help them determine what actually had taken place. One of the investigators, Jack Ferguson, had heard about my work. He contacted me and we arranged to meet in Georgia for Dennis' hypnotic interrogation.

I had an inkling that Dennis was suffering from traumatic amnesia. The shock of his mother's sudden disappearance, along with any foul play he might have been witness to, I reasoned, could have caused him to erase all memory of the events of the first two days of her absence.

Ferguson and I commandeered the warden's office and tape recorder at the Georgia penitentiary where Dennis was incarcerated. As soon as the convict was brought in, I could tell he was nervous, though he appeared solemn, stoic, a man of few words. I offered my often repeated explanation of what he was about to undergo, in an effort to put him at ease. It must have done the trick because he went under easily. It took just a few trial questions, though, to realize Dennis was the kind of subject who frequently answers with no more than a cryptic "yes" or "no." As hypnosis went about its work, however, memories that had been buried for eight years were unearthed slowly but surely.

I tested Dennis' recall of those crucial events in the distant past with a simple question: "You remember the last time you saw your mother, don't you, Dennis?"

A brief "uh-huh" was all Dennis would allow in response.

"When was that?" I persisted.

"About nine-thirty."

"Nine-thirty when?"

"Thursday night."

"And what was happening?"

"She was going somewhere."

"Were you with her?"

"Yeah, I was getting out of the car."

"And where was this?"

"Farmingdale, in front of the house."

"In front of your house?"

"Yeah."

"Did you go into the house then?"

"Yeah."

"Did your mother drive away?"

"Yeah."

"You told the investigators that was the last time you saw her, is that right?"

"Right."

"Okay, now you walk into the house. What do you do?"

"Went into the kitchen."

"What are you doing in the kitchen?"

"Getting something to eat."

"What are you eating?"

"A sandwich."

"Fine. What happens now?"

"Go into the living room and watch TV."

"What time are you going to go to bed?"

"After the movie."

"Are you watching the movie in your mind?"

"Yeah."

"What is the movie?"

"A Western."

"Tell me what happens now. The movie's over . . ."

Dennis hesitated a few moments before replying, "I go upstairs and go to bed."

"Go ahead."

"I go to sleep."

"Now you're sleeping, right? You're fourteen years old. It's November 8, 1970. Your mother let you out of the car. You came into the house, had a sandwich, watched television, went to bed. Now you're sleeping. What happens then?"

Dennis was breathing heavily. He seemed to be searching his mind and grew slightly agitated as he answered, "I wake up. There's an argument."

"Go ahead."

"There's a lot of hollering."

"Who's hollering?"

"Mother and father."

"What are they hollering about?"

"My little sister and brother."

"Tell me about it."

"He says he's going to Massachusetts. She says, 'Don't take the kids.'"

"Go ahead."

"They're just arguing."

"Are you afraid?"

"Yes."

"Why?"

"I don't know."

"Is your heart beating fast?"

"Yeah."

"Have you heard your mother and father arguing before?"

"Yes."

"Have they argued about going to Massachusetts before?"

"No."

"Okay, now what happens?"

"I get up and go downstairs. I see him hit her."

"You see who hit who?"

"My father hit my mother."

"With what?"

"His hand."

"Which hand?"

"Right hand."

"What happens then?"

"I run back upstairs."

"I want you to see yourself downstairs, Dennis. I want you to see your father hit your mother. What does your mother do now?"

"Falls on the floor."

"Is she crying?"

"No."

"What is she doing?"

"Just lying there."

"Does your father say anything?"

"No."

"Does he say anything to you?"

"No."

"Does he see you?"

"No."

"Then you go back upstairs?"

"Yes."

"Are the other children upstairs?"

"Yes."

"Are they awake?"

"No."

"Do you wake them up?"

"No."

"What do you do now?"

"Get back in bed."

"Do you hear anything then?"

"Nothing."

"Do you go to sleep right away?"

"No."

"How long do you stay awake?"

"A long time."

"All the time you stay awake, do you hear anything?"

"No."

"Nothing?"

"No."

"When you're upstairs, can you usually hear noises downstairs?"

"A little bit."

"And this night, as you lie there under the covers, can you hear anything?"

"No."

"What happens next?"

Dennis' heavy breathing was the only sound that could be heard in the office. I waited a few moments, but he didn't answer the question. "What time do you awaken in the morning?" I continued.

"I don't know. It's dark out."

"It's dark out, huh? What do you do?"

"Get up and go downstairs."

"What do you see?"

"Nothing."

"Do you see your father?"

"No."

"Your mother?"

"No."

"What do you do now?"

"Go into the kitchen."

"Okay, you're in the kitchen. You're fourteen years old and it's dark out. What do you do?"

"Make coffee."

"Uh-huh, go ahead."

"Drink the coffee."

"You're doing very well, Dennis. Keep going."

"Went out."

"Where do you go?"

"Just walk around."

"What time is it?"

"I don't know."

"Where do you walk to?"

"Out in the woods, back of the house."

"Do you usually go there?"

"No."

"Why do you go there today?"

"Just wanted to get out."

"Do you see anybody?"

"No."

"Are you walking in the woods now?"

"No."

"Where are you?"

"The road on the other side of the woods."

"On the other side? How far from your house?"

"I don't know."

"Half a mile?"

"Less."

"Football field?"

"Maybe."

"What do you do there?"

"Just start walking."

"Where do you walk to? Tell me about it."

"Just walk."

"See yourself there walking along. What are you thinking about?"

"My mother."

"Is it getting light yet?"

"No."

"Where are you now?"

"In front of a big house."

"Whose house is it?"

"I don't know."

"Have you ever seen it before?"

"No."

"Is it in your town?"

"I don't know."

"What do you do there?"

"Just look at the house."

"Then what do you do?"

"Go in the woods."

"Now what?"

"Don't know."

"See yourself walking through the woods. Eventually you come to another place. Where is that?"

After a long pause, Dennis answered, "Go to the road."

"Same road?"

"No."

"Where does this road lead you to?"

"Town."

"Which town?"

"Bedford."

"Is it light yet?"

"Yeah."

"What are you doing in Bedford?"

"Just walking."

"Where are you walking to?"

"Madison."

"All right, you arrive in Madison . . ."

Dennis nodded.

"What do you do there?"

"Go to a bar."

"Which bar?"

"The . . . White Horse."

"Is anybody in there?"

"No."

"Is the bartender there?"

"No, it's closed."

"What do you do then?"

"Walk."

"Is it early in the morning now?"

"No."

"What time is it?"

"I don't know . . . late morning."

"Are you walking a long ways?"

"Yes."

"How far is the White Horse from your house?"

"I don't know."

"Five miles?"

"More."

"You walked a long way then. Ten miles?"

"More."

"You really covered a lot of territory. How do you feel now?"

"Good."

"Okay, now you leave the White Horse. Where are you going?"

"Home."

"You walked all the way back home?"

"No."

"Where do you go?"

"Get a ride."

"Who picked you up?"

"A lady."

"What's her name?"

"Don't know."

"Where's she going?"

"Don't know."

"Did she take you right to your house?"

"No."

"Where does she take you?"

"The post office."

"The post office in what town?"

"Danford."

"Okay, you're at the post office. What do you do now?"

"Walk across the bridge."

"Is it a nice day?"

"It's night."

"Oh, it's night now. Okay, when you walk across the bridge, where do you go?"

"To the house."

"Your house?"

"Yes."

"Now do you enter the house? Do you go in the front door?"

"Don't go in."

"What do you do?"

"Look in the window."

"Who's in there?"

"Father, sister, and brother."

"Are you afraid?"

"Yes."

"Why?"

"Don't know."

"What do you do now?"

"Go in the back door."

"Go ahead."

"I go into the kitchen. Turn around and go back out."

"Why?"

"Looking for Mother."

"Where do you go now?"

"Out to Mother's car."

"What do you do there?"

"Go in. Go to sleep."

"Do you see anybody while you're in the house? I mean do you talk to anybody?"

"No."

"Does anybody see you?"

"No."

"Do you hear anybody talking?"

"My father."

"What is he saying?"

"Telling the children to go to bed."

"Does anybody say anything about your mother?"

"No."

"Okay, you're sleeping in the car. Is it cold?"

"Yes."

"How long do you sleep?"

"I don't know."

"Do you hear anything while you're sleeping in the car?"

"No."

"Do you see anything or anybody?"

"No."

"Tell me when you wake up."

"Morning."

"Morning now? What do you do?"

"Go back in the woods."

"While you're in the car, do you do anything besides sleep?"

"No."

"Do you look in the glove compartment or under the front seat?"

"Look in the compartment."

"What are you looking for?"

"I don't know. Just looking."

"Do you find anything?"

"No."

"Do you write anything while you're in the car?"

Dennis was silent for a few seconds. Finally he said, "Don't remember."

"Okay, let's go back. Just go back in your mind now as you relax more and more. Take a deep breath and let it out slowly. Let yourself go into a deeper relaxation. You're fourteen. You've just been walking all day and part of the night before. You come home. You look in the window. You're worried. You're afraid. You see your father, sister, and brother. You go around the house and into the back door. You don't see your mother. You go back outside and walk to the car. See yourself there, a frightened boy. Is the door unlocked . . . on the car?"

"Yes."

"See yourself getting into the car. See the interior of that car. You remember the car well. Try to capture the smell. See yourself there and see the things you do and tell me about them."

Dennis didn't answer. He was grappling with the innermost locked gate of his amnesia: the note found in the car. I knew if I didn't proceed with care, the memory of writing it—presuming he did so—might remain firmly blocked from his conscious mind.

"Dennis, what do you do when you get in the car?" I continued.

"I just sit."

"Are you crying?"

"No."

"Are you worried?"

"Yes."

"Do you know why you're worried?"

"No."

"What are you doing in the car now?"

"Looking out the window."

"What do you see?"

"My father."

"Where is he?"

"In the kitchen."

"What's he doing?"

"Sitting at the table."

"Is anybody with him?"

"No."

"What do you do now?"

"Lay down and go to sleep."

"Now there comes a time when you wake up. Tell me about that."

"Look out the window."

"Is it daytime?"

"Yes."

"What do you do?"

"Look around inside the car."

"What do you see?"

"A book."

"What do you do now?"

"Open up the glove box."

"What's in there?"

"Papers."

"Do you look through them?"

"No."

"Do you take anything out of the glove box?"

"Piece of paper."

"What's on the piece of paper?"

"Nothing."

"What do you do with it?"

Dennis thought for a moment and then said, "Write on it."

"What do you write on it?"

There was a long pause. Dennis was trembling slightly. "Kill," he said very softly.

"Kill?" Here at last was the breakthrough we had been working toward. I felt like I had just made it to the top of Everest.

"Yes," Dennis answered.

"What else?"

"Father kill."

"What does that mean, Dennis?"

"Father hurt Mother."

"How much did he hurt her?"

"I don't know."

"Why do you write, 'kill'?"

"I don't know."

"Do you write anything else on that paper?"

"No."

"What do you do with it?"

"Throw it on the floor of the car."

"All right, what do you do now?"

"Get out of the car and go to the woods."

"What do you do in the woods?"

"Sit down."

"Is it early morning now?"

"No, afternoon."

"Are you thinking about what you should do?"

"Yes."

"What do you decide?"

"Go to the house."

"Are you going into the house now?"

"Yes."

"Do you see anybody when you go into the house?"

"No, nobody home."

"Do you go upstairs?"

"Yes."

"Nobody's upstairs either?"

"No."

"What do you do?"

"Lay down on the bed. Go to sleep."

"When do you awaken?"

"Morning."

"What do you do now?"

"Get up and go downstairs."

"What do you see?"

"Father making coffee."

"What do you do?"

"Talk to my father."

"What do you say?"

"He asks me where I was. . . . I tell him I walked in the woods."

"What's the rest of the conversation?"

"I ask him where Mother is. . . . Tells me she isn't home. I go out. . . . Go to the store."

"What store is that, Dennis?"

"Down the road."

"What kind of a store is it?"

"Small candy store."

"Do you buy anything?"

"No."

"What do you do there?"

"Look for my friend . . . Danny."

"Is he there?"

"No."

"What do you do now?"

"Go back home."

"Do you go in the house?"

"Yes."

"Who's there?"

"Father, sister, and brother."

"Do you talk to your father?"

"No."

"What do you do?"

"Sit down and watch TV."

"How long do you stay there?"

"Half an hour."

"What time is it now?"

"Morning . . . late morning."

"What do you do then?"

"Decide to go to Aunt Harriet's house."

"How do you get there?"

"Father takes me in his car."

"Do you go into Aunt Harriet's house?"

"Yes."

"Does your father?"

"Yes."

"And what happens there?"

"He leaves."

"Before he leaves, does he talk to Harriet about your mother?"

"Don't know."

"You're there, aren't you?"

"Yes . . . in the other room."

"Can you hear them talking?"

"No."

"Now your father leaves Harriet's house. What do you do?"

"Watch TV."

"What is Harriet doing?"

"Talking to Cathy."

"Who else is there?"

"Ronny."

"You and Cathy, Ronny, and Harriet?"

"Kevin."

"Kevin also? Five people are there?"

"Right."

"Where does your father go?"

"I don't know."

"What else happens?"

"Father tells Harriet he's going to Massachusetts."

"What does Harriet say about that?"

"She asks me where Mother is. . . . I tell her I don't know. . . . She isn't home. Car is there. She isn't."

"Then what?"

Dennis didn't answer.

"Does she ask you where your mother went?"

"Yes."

"What do you say?"

"Don't know."

"How long do you stay in Harriet's house?"

"I don't know . . . two hours."

"Then what happens?"

"Harriet . . . calls someone."

"Who?"

"I don't know."

"What does she talk about?"

"She wants somebody to stay with the kids."

"What for?"

"She wants to go to my house to look around."

"Why would she be doing that?"

"Don't know. She wants to."

"Look around for what?"

"Don't know."

"All right, I want you to back up a bit to when Harriet asks you where your mother is. See yourself talking to her when she says, 'Where's your mother?' and you say, 'She isn't home.'"

"Yes."

"Does Harriet question you any further on that?"

"She asks me when I saw her last."

"Tell me all about that conversation. You're really doing a great job, Dennis."

"I say I saw her last night."

"Do you tell Harriet about the fight your mother and father had?"

"No."

"Why not?"

"Don't know."

"Did anybody tell you not to say anything about the fight?"

"No."

"But you don't tell Harriet?"

"No."

"So after you tell Harriet that your mother isn't home but you don't know where she is, Harriet calls somebody to stay with the kids. Is that right?"

"Yes."

"And then what happens?"

"We go to my house."

"How do you get there?"

"Harriet drives."

"All right, Dennis, see yourself in front of the house. Who's in the car?"

"Just me and Harriet."

"And you both go into your house?"

"Yes."

"Now you're in the house. Who's home?"

"Nobody."

"What do you do and what do you say to each other? Tell me about that."

"Harriet goes into the living room. I make some coffee. . . . She comes back with Mother's clothes. She asks me where her bathrobe is. . . . We look for the bathrobe. Don't find it."

"Go ahead."

"Somebody comes."

"How do you know somebody comes?"

"Hear the back door open."

"Then what?"

"Somebody's talking."

"To you?"

"No, to Aunt Harriet."

"A man or a woman?"

"A woman."

"What are they saying?"

"Something about Mother."

"Who is this woman?"

"Landlady."

"And what are they saying about your mother?"

"She hasn't been home for two days."

"The landlady is telling Harriet that your mother hasn't been home for two days?"

"Yes."

"Who is the landlady?"

"A neighbor, Mrs. Guardino."

"What else do they say about your mother besides the fact that she hasn't been home for two days?"

"Nothing."

"They must have said something else. Let's hear that conversation. What do they say?"

No response from Dennis.

"Can you recall some more of that conversation?" I insisted.

"No."

"You were looking for the bathrobe with Harriet just a few minutes ago. Did you go in the room where your mother slept?"

"Yes."

"What did you see there?"

"Nothing."

"Wasn't there anything in the room—a dresser . . . ?"

"Yes . . . a daybed . . . TV . . . chairs, table."

"Very good. Now as you look at the daybed, Dennis, can you see what's on it?"

"Blanket, pillow."

"Anything else?"

"No."

"Can you tell if there's anything under the blanket?"

"No."

"Can you tell if the mattress is still on the bed?"

"Yes."

"How can you tell?"

"Blanket is tucked under it."

In the original investigation of this case, the Farmingdale police had noted that the mattress was missing from Ruth McCormick's bed. But apparently it was still there when Dennis returned to the house with his mother's sister.

I decided to shift the questioning back to Mrs. Guardino.

"Now the landlady comes in and talks to Harriet. Which room are they talking in?"

"The kitchen."

"And which room are you in while they're talking?"

"Living room."

"About how long do they talk?"

"Ten minutes."

"And then what happens?"

"Comes into the living room."

"Who?"

"Mrs. Guardino."

"And she talks to you?"

"She asks me about Mother."

"Tell me all about that conversation."

"She asks me where Mother is. I say I don't know."

"Go ahead."

"She asks me when I saw her last . . . last night."

"Okay, she goes after that?"

"Yes."

"But Harriet is still there?"

"Yes."

"What happens now?"

"Look for more clothes."

"And what do you find?"

"Everything."

"By everything, you mean you find all your mother's clothes?"

"Yes."

"I think you said before that the bathrobe was missing. Is that right?"

"Yes."

"Is there anything else missing?"

"A coat."

"What else?"

"Nothing."

"Good. You're really doing a tremendous job, Dennis. I'm proud of you. Now while these memories are coming back to you so well, I just want you to go . . . to backtrack a bit to when you come down the stairs, when you hear your mother and father arguing and you see your father hit your mother. Do you have that in your mind now?"

"Yes."

"What is your mother wearing?"

"Bathrobe."

"What else?"

"Coat."

"What about her hair? Does she have anything on her head?"

"No."

"What is her hair like? Can you tell me?"

"Long, wavy."

"Is that how it is when your father hits her?"

"Yes."

"All right. Now you say that after your father strikes your mother, she doesn't cry out or anything. Is that right?"

"Yes."

"Tell me again what she does."

"Falls down."

"Is there any blood?"

"Don't know."

"Why don't you know?"

"Father's in the way."

"What's your father wearing?"

"Dark pants."

"What else?"

"Blue shirt."

"Long sleeves?"

"Yes."

"Where are they standing when he hits her?"

"By daybed."

"The daybed is where . . . in which room?"

"Mother's bedroom, downstairs."

"And where does she fall?"

"On the bed and then the floor."

"You've done a superlative job, Dennis. I'm going to take a little break now. Maybe we'll hypnotize you again a little later. If we do it again, you'll find that you'll be able to go under much quicker, much deeper, because hypnosis is a learning process. The more you practice it, the better you become at it, just like anything else.

"Now I'm going to count back from three to one, and you

just follow along with me. When you open your eyes, you're
going to feel wonderful. You're going to be able to remember
everything. It's all right for you to remember at this time. Okay
now, three, get ready . . . two, roll your eyes up. . . . Do it
now . . . and one, slowly let your eyes open, feeling perfect in
every way."

Dennis opened his eyes, blinked a few times, yawned and
stretched.

"Was that relaxing?" I asked.

"Sure was."

"That's what it is all right."

Dennis seemed pleased with himself and a lot more at ease than
he had been at the beginning of the interrogation. He told me he
was amazed at what he had just experienced. He had always harbored the suspicion that his stepfather had harmed his mother in
some way and was responsible for her disappearance, but he
never knew for certain, at least not consciously. The loss of his
mother was the most unhappy and frustrating event of his life,
he said, and he was glad he could put the matter to rest at last.

The convict spoke with a soft, southern drawl. It was only
then I realized that all the while he was under hypnosis, his
speech had reverted to the clipped, sharper sounds characteristic
of the New England states—the way he had spoken during his
childhood, at the time of the events he was reliving, before he
had moved to the South.

By some stroke of luck, Dennis was an exceptional hypnotic
subject. With little work on my part, he fell into an especially
deep trance. His altered speech pattern and his use of the present
tense during the interview, without prompting, are clues to the
intensity with which he was reliving long-ago events. I included
the complete transcript of our dialogue here, not only to make
this point, but also to show how hypnosis can draw out the
memory of a traumatic experience from even the most tight-
lipped subject, when the interrogation is done with skill and persistence.

No further hypnosis was necessary. Jack Ferguson got more
than he had hoped for. He confronted Roy McCormick with
Dennis' hypnotic revelations and advised him to come clean regarding the true circumstances of his wife's disappearance. The

jig was up; the man was up against a wall. He had no recourse but to reveal the guilt he had carefully concealed for more than eight years.

McCormick explained that on that fateful night, his wife had come home drunk. They had an argument. In a moment of fury, he beat her, he confessed to Ferguson, but he didn't mean to kill her. When he realized what he had done, he panicked. He hauled his wife's body to his car, put it in the trunk, drove to a secluded spot, and buried it. A few days later, he moved all of his belongings and Ruth's children to Massachusetts. He also took along his wife's bloodstained mattress and burned it when he got to his destination.

Ferguson wanted McCormick to show him where he had buried the body. The man agreed to take him to the spot, but he must have known that if the body were found, he would be arrested on a charge of manslaughter. Ferguson brought McCormick to Rhode Island where the suspect proceeded to take the detective on a statewide wild goose chase, indicating one place after another where he thought he had deposited his wife's body. At each location, nothing was found.

To date, the whereabouts of Ruth McCormick's burial plot remains a mystery. Until her body is found, Roy McCormick is a free man.

Another case that pitted my hypnotic skills against traumatic amnesia was a savage homicide that took place in Brooklyn in 1977. While it wasn't necessary to bridge a gap of many years to achieve a breakthrough in this instance, the vicious crime's lone witness was, ironically, a fourteen-year-old boy.

It was close to midnight on a cold, wet night just a few days after Christmas. Falling temperatures threatened to turn the puddles and slush remaining from the day's snowfall into a covering of slippery ice.

Young Henri Rodin was unpacking cartons of cereal boxes in the back room of his uncle Claude's small neighborhood grocery store. He could hear the whooshing sound of an occasional car plowing through the slush on Flatbush Avenue as his thoughts wandered to the few days remaining of his Christmas vacation.

He still hadn't tried out his new skateboard, the most prized of his holiday gifts, and he longed for at least one day of dry sidewalks before school started.

He liked living in the city and was happy to be in America. His French-born parents had immigrated to this country when he was a baby.

He glanced at the small clock his uncle Claude kept on one of the shelves. Just one more hour and they would be closing up shop. As he overheard his uncle chatting amiably with the last of the day's customers, he hoped that, when he got home, his parents would let him stay up awhile to listen to some of his new records.

Suddenly he heard shouts and scuffling. He rushed out, looked to the front of the store, and saw his uncle standing in his usual spot behind the register in a white shirt and familiar waist-tied white apron. Facing him across the counter were two men, one with what looked like a huge rifle aimed directly at his uncle's chest.

"Go back into the storeroom!" his uncle yelled.

"No, get down on the floor," the man with the gun commanded.

The other rushed over and pushed Henri down hard until he was lying flat on his stomach. "Stay there and keep your mouth shut," he growled.

Henri could feel his heart pounding. The idea that the store might be robbed someday had occurred to him, but the thought that it was happening right now while he was alone with his uncle made him sick to his stomach with fear. Lying where he was, all he could see were the feet of the intruders. He prayed that they would leave without harming him or his uncle.

"Give me the fucking money," he heard one of the men demand. He could hear the sound of the cash drawer opening and his uncle fumbling through the bills and coins.

"Is that all you've got?" said the man with the gun. "Give me the rest."

"There isn't any more," he heard his uncle plead with fear in his voice.

He had hardly finished the sentence when the gunman said, "This is for you."

Henri heard what sounded to him like the clicking of a bolt action. Suddenly, there was a sharp explosion, the loudest noise he had ever experienced. Its violent reverberations sliced through his body and the floor beneath it. Then came the crashing sound of bottles and cans falling and a muffled thud, as if his uncle had collapsed.

The thieves ran from the store and Henri remained frozen on the floor. He sobbed and called his uncle's name but got no response. His mind was so filled with dread at what he would find if he got up and looked that he couldn't move.

It seemed much longer to Henri, but it was only a matter of seconds after the gunfire when Jack Dougherty, the friendly proprietor of the bar and grill next door, rushed into the store. The comfort of his presence restored movement to Henri's body, but he was sobbing and trembling and unable to respond to Mr. Dougherty's questioning.

The saloonkeeper brought the boy next door and quickly returned to survey the scene. For the first time, he noticed blood spattered all over the cash register and the counter that supported it. He looked down behind it and recoiled in horror. There lying on his back amid cans and broken glass was a lifeless Claude Rodin. Where his chest used to be was a gaping, bloody hole—the kind of wound that could be made only by the ravaging buckshot of a shotgun fired at close range.

When Detective Mike Walsh arrived on the scene, he questioned Henri but the boy was so traumatized that he couldn't tell Mike what the men looked like, what the gun looked like, or anything at all about the incident.

Weeks went by and Mike continued his investigation of the case but he couldn't come up with anything. He had little to go on. It had occurred to him that he should bring Henri to see me, in the hope that hypnosis would succeed in getting at least a description from him. But the boy's parents were apprehensive about subjecting him to the procedure. They were pleased that Henri was beginning to return to his normal self and preferred to leave well enough alone.

Finally, three months after the crime, I succeeded in convincing Henri's parents that hypnotizing the boy offered the only hope of ever finding his uncle's killer. I assured them that the hypnotic interview would be harmless, and that releasing Henri's repressed memories of the incident would actually be the best thing we could do for him.

We brought the boy over to the department's Psychological Services Unit. I could tell he was frightened, but I succeeded in getting him to relax by talking to him about school and about his latest skateboard maneuvers.

Detective John McGrath, working with me at the time, actually performed the hypnosis. The technique he used was one we had put together when the program was in its infancy.

He said to the already hypnotized boy, "Let your mind go back, back in time. Now it's March. Go back to February, then January. Now it's December 28, a day you'll never forget. Just allow the memories that are in the subconscious mind to flow out in a smooth and effortless manner, and begin by telling us where you were when the men came in."

"I don't remember any men coming in . . . uh . . . I think I was in the back room. Yeah, it was almost closing time."

"Okay, you're in the back room. What happens now?"

"I came out. There was a man . . . no, two men and one was holding a big gun. But I can't tell you any more. I can't remember."

"Just relax, Henri, relax. Go back in your mind now. You're standing in the store. Look at the man holding the rifle. Start with the top of his head, and as well as you can, tell us what he looks like."

The boy took a deep breath and then sat motionless for what seemed like several minutes, although I am sure it was no more than thirty seconds. Just as I was about to tell McGrath that we should take a break and try again later, I noticed a subtle relaxation of tension in Henri's face. A split second after that, he spoke, but much faster and with more assurance than before.

"He had no hair. His head was completely bald but he had a mustache. He was black but not really black—more like tan. He was real tall—my uncle's head came up to his shoulder—and skinny, sort of like a basketball player . . ."

At that point, Detective Walsh very quietly came over to me from where he was sitting and whispered in my ear, "I know who this guy is. I know exactly who he is."

He reached into his briefcase and pulled out a folder containing mug shots of possible suspects. He held one up to me, making sure that neither Henri nor McGrath could see what he was doing.

I had to admit to myself that the man in the picture fit Henri's description perfectly.

When my attention returned to hypnotist and subject, McGrath had succeeded in getting Henri to recall details of the gunman's dress and manner of speech, and of the gun itself. He had described its bolt action, but we so rarely ran across that kind of shotgun that we were certain he was mistaken. McGrath was wrapping up the session by congratulating the boy on his keen memory and thanking him for his co-operation.

Henri came out of the trance smiling and relieved. There was no hysteria and no anger.

Mike Walsh consulted the BCI file in which the department strives to keep track of everyone who has been arrested and what their present status is. He discovered that the suspect whose picture fit Henri's description had since been arrested for another crime and had served time in the Suffolk County jail.

Mike brought Henri out there to take a look at some photographs. The Suffolk police have an excellent setup for displaying mug shots. The advanced system is capable of projecting a criminal's photographic image in 3D while playing back a recording of his or her voice.

After the boy had looked at about thirty pictures, Mike slipped in the shot of the man he had a hunch about. "That's him!" Henri shouted. He was unshakably certain about it.

The gunman was arrested. Hidden at the back of a closet in his apartment, much to our surprise, was a bolt-action shotgun. This guy's partner was found. Both men confessed to the grocery store robbery/homicide, and some months later, a third man involved in the crime—the driver of the car for the others—was arrested.

5

AN IMAGE RECORDED

In describing the role of hypnosis in criminal investigation, I find myself emphasizing over and over again, during seminars and interviews, that hypnotic interrogation must work hand in hand with other investigative aids. It should never be regarded as a source of unquestionable fact. It won't do the job by itself, but coupled with other means of gathering evidence, it becomes a potent force that can help make the task of accurately reconstructing a crime a lot quicker and easier.

In the investigations I have worked on, the one forensic tool that seems to crop up most often as a hypnosis partner is the drawing of composites. The relationship is a natural one. Both depend on witnesses' and victims' memory. And since there is absolutely no doubt that hypnosis can enhance memory, then it comes as no surprise that it is frequently called on to help people provide us with better renderings of suspects' faces.

My initial strategy in dealing with the challenge of capturing a subject's memories on paper was to have the composite artist right there during the hypnosis session. At an appropriate time during the questioning, I would say to the subject, "When I count to three, gently open your eyes, but remain in this deeply relaxed state. Look at what the artist is doing and see if it resembles the person you're describing. Talk to the artist about any changes he should make," and so on. But this was a difficult arrangement for everyone concerned. It was asking too much of the artist to set aside a couple of hours in his schedule to stand by during a hypnotic interrogation. And it was demanding on the subject to have to open his eyes in the middle of a trance. There was always the risk of disturbing his relaxation.

I decided early on that keeping the two interviews separate was a much better setup. What we do now is schedule the witness' composite session as soon after his hypnotic experience as possible. I found that once a person's memory is boosted by hypnosis, the charge carries over for a period of time. If the witness goes to the artist later in the day or even the next day, we get just as much heightened recall as we would if he were giving his description under hypnosis. The trance experience helps the mind etch a remembered image in sharp relief. The imprint is still there for the witness to reflect on during his exchange with the artist.

Contrary to popular belief, a composite sketch doesn't have to be a faithful rendering of the suspect's face for it to have some value in an investigation. It is not meant to be a portrait. True, the more the drawing resembles the suspected perpetrator—and hypnotic recall improves the odds by a wide margin—the better the likelihood of apprehending him. But if, at most, the sketch calls attention to a distinguishing feature—a scar, a bald head, a prominent nose—it can still be enormously helpful. What composites do best, in the end, is narrow the field for the investigators. As an obvious example, if a number of suspects are being considered and the drawing depicts a man with dark hair and eyes and a mustache, then all clean-shaven, light-eyed blonds can be eliminated.

One of the cases I worked on that focuses on this composite-hypnosis partnership was the murder at the Metropolitan Opera

House of violinist Helen Hagnes. Among the most celebrated cases on record, the brutal sexual assault and homicide instigated the largest police investigation mounted in New York in recent years. A task force of twenty-five to thirty investigators was put into action and headquartered right at the scene of the crime, the backstage of the mammoth opera house. The list of possible suspects and witnesses numbered nearly two thousand. These included the Met's behind-the-scenes personnel and members of the Berlin Ballet, which was playing a limited engagement at the house at the time of the murder. The investigators had the herculean task of questioning all of these people about their whereabouts before, during, and after the assault, and when they last saw the victim. Keeping records of depositions and checking alibis added to the enormous undertaking.

Helen Hagnes was a free-lance violinist married to sculptor Janis Mintiks. She was an attractive thirty-year-old, who was respected as a dependable, accomplished musician by members of her profession. She had been contracted to play with other free-lancers like herself in an orchestra that had been pieced together for the German company's tour. Her untimely death came at around 10 P.M. on the night of July 23, 1980, while, onstage, dancers leaped and pirouetted to the delight of the packed house.

The second ballet on the program ended at about nine-thirty. The third selection was to be danced to recorded music, so members of the orchestra were free to relax until they were needed again for the last number. Miss Hagnes headed backstage, after volunteering to a fellow musician that she wanted to find Valery Panov's dressing room. The celebrated Russian dancer had just performed a pas de deux with his wife Galina and was not scheduled, that particular evening, to be onstage again. Miss Hagnes had a business proposition for him. She thought he might be interested in commissioning a likeness of himself to be sculpted by her husband.

The comely musician never returned to the orchestra pit. Her absence was a baffling mystery until the next morning when a woman's nude and bound body was found on a ledge close to the bottom of an air shaft behind the recesses of the Met's great stage.

Later that day, even before the shocking headlines hit the front pages of the New York dailies, I got a call from Richard

Nicastro, Chief of Detectives in Manhattan. He told me he had questioned a member of the Berlin company who said she had seen a woman fitting Miss Hagnes' description backstage at the time the third ballet was in progress. The young ballerina, an American named Laura Cutler, was sure the violinist was with a man who looked like a worker of some kind. This was the only lead the chief had at that point and he was hot to get as accurate a description of the man as possible. He was counting on hypnosis to sharpen Miss Cutler's memory.

He asked me to come to the Met that afternoon. But when he volunteered that Miss Cutler was in a state of severe anxiety and exhaustion, I recommended waiting a few days until she was in better shape. The chief agreed, but the very next day, July 25, I got my orders to get over there right away.

My assistant, Detective Millie Markman, went with me. We met with Detective Jerry Giorgio of the Manhattan Homicide Task Force, Detective Heaney of the 28th PDU, and Miss Cutler in a small, private room in the maze of backstage facilities. The dancer was understandably tired and upset. I did my best to put her at ease. But I was feeling the pressure of the awesome investigation and wasted no time in getting the proceedings underway. I began the interview at 1540 hours.

Before hypnotizing Laura, I asked her to tell me as much as she could about the series of events that led up to meeting Miss Hagnes. The dancer's recollections of where she had gone and what she did were related with assurance. Her memory was strong on detail, all the better for hypnosis. When describing the man she thought was with Miss Hagnes, her confidence waned. She wasn't getting a clear enough picture. I asked her how old he appeared to be. Somewhere between thirty-five and forty, she estimated.

My introductory remarks to Laura about hypnosis were sprinkled with praise for her keen memory. I told her it would be even better once she was hypnotized, and that she would have no trouble seeing a perfect mind's-eye image of the man we were all interested in.

The young performer had good arm levitation in the HIP. She went under quickly with the eye-roll induction, and was a rather responsive subject over all. The only problem was that she spoke in such a soft whisper, her remarks were barely audible. I had to keep moving the recorder mike closer to her mouth. When I was certain she was in a nice, deep trance and sufficiently relaxed, I began the questioning we hoped would lead to Helen Hagnes' killer.

"What time do you arrive at the Met for your performance, Laura?"

"I got there about seven-thirty."

"Where are you coming from?"

"I just had dinner at the Café Deux with a cousin and her fiancé. They were going to see the performance."

"And what are you having for dinner?"

"I had scrod with potatoes, with tomato soup."

I noted that Laura's voice had a hint of a foreign accent to it, no doubt the result of living in Europe for a number of years. I reminded her, "I want you to remember to talk to me in the present tense, okay? Is this a happy dinner you're having?"

"Yes, happy. I'm a little nervous."

"Why is that?"

"Because I haven't seen this cousin. She's a girl, twenty-eight."

"I see."

"But she's very nice and we're all relaxed."

"Are they going to watch you perform?"

"They are."

"Now you're finished dinner. You're going to the opera house, right?"

"Yes."

"How are you getting there?"

"We're walking. It's very close."

"I see. What kind of evening is it?"

"The weather is nice. It's not too hot. There's a breeze."

"About what time is it now?"

"It's about seven twenty-five."

"What happens when you get to the opera house?"

"We part inside the lobby by the escalator. I tell them I hope they enjoy the show and I'll call my aunt. She wasn't able to come. I leave them. I walk down the stairs."

"Do you have a costume change now?"

"Yes, I have to get ready. I'm in the first ballet. I go through the doors to the garage area. There are people coming in who are going to the show. I enter at the stage entrance. I walk in and Hans is there. He's one of the principal dancers. He's dancing tonight. We arrive at the same time and we speak. I tell him he must dance well because I have friends in the audience. He goes off to the right where his dressing room is and I continue through another door, through a hallway to the left. I immediately turn right into the dressing room."

"Okay, fine. I'd like you to review what happens next in your mind's eye. You don't have to tell me everything. I want you to see yourself changing, leaving the dressing room, going onto the stage, performing your part in the ballet. Tell me when you reach the part where you're onstage performing."

I waited a minute or two while Laura retraced her steps. "Are you there yet?"

"Almost."

"Almost? Fine. Now you're onstage and you're dancing?"

"Yes."

"And your friends are in the audience?"

"Yes."

"How do you feel?"

"I feel all right. What I have to do is very easy."

"I see. Are you doing it well?"

"Not badly. I have just one problem. I ate dinner too soon before the performance. Now I have to be careful about my stomach."

"I see. Now you complete your part in the ballet and leave. Do you go and change your clothes?"

"No."

"What do you do?"

"I go directly back to the dressing room and take my costume off. I decide to leave my hair up because I think I'll go down to the ballet studio and work. I was finished for the evening but I had to wait for my friends who were staying until the end of the performance. So I put on leotards, some socks, sweat pants, and soft shoes. And then I talk with the other girls."

"You're in leotards now?"

"Yes."

"Where are you?"

"I'm in the dressing room. I'm thinking that before I go downstairs to work, I'll just go backstage and watch for a little while because the Panovs are performing. So I go back to the stage."

"Are you there now?"

"Yes."

"Can you see the Panovs?"

"Yes."

"How are they doing?"

"All right."

"Do you think they've done better before?"

"Yes. She's doing better than he is. I'm standing next to one of the extras who's in a dress suit because he has to give flowers at the end of the act. He's asking me why Valery, that's Panov, is wearing black tights. It doesn't look right with the act. I tell him I was wondering the same thing myself."

"Doesn't he always wear black tights?"

"The first night he wore white."

"I see."

"The extra says it's odd, but the black tights make him look fatter, which isn't normal for black."

"Can you see them clearly dancing now?"

"Yes."

"Okay, what do you do now?"

"Other dancers are waiting because they go on directly after the pas de deux. . . . The Panovs are finished and they go off. They go to the side of the stage opposite from where I'm standing."

"What do you do now?"

"I'm still standing back there watching the other dancers. They're taking off leg warmers, knitted socks. . . . The stage manager is a girl. She calls for the curtain to go up, the lights to go off, and then for the tape to start. It does and they begin. There are five sections to this ballet. I watch all this—the first dance, the second, the third is a solo. Hans dances very well. The fourth dance begins with two boys. I've already watched this whole ballet. I think, well, if I'm going to go to the ballet studio I'd better go now. It's getting late. So I start to leave. I glance back over the stage manager's desk where the clock is. It's about a quarter to ten. I was thinking it was a bit late to go to work but I decided I would anyway. I walk back and leave the stage area. The studio is on the cellar level. I don't know which way to go."

"Don't try to remember. See yourself leaving the stage area. You look at the clock by the manager's desk. It's about a quarter to ten. Where are you walking now?"

"I'm walking through to the side stage—the way to the door I have to get to. I'm going the route that takes me further from the stage. I go through sets which are stored on the side, and then I'm walking through the door that leads to the hallway. There's a water fountain to my left. But I don't take any water. I go straight to the elevator and press the button because I'm in a hurry."

"What happens now?"

"I wait. It seems to take a long time. After a few seconds, these people walk up. The woman . . . She could be thirty, not much older. She was wearing black. She's talking to a man who's walking with her. Somehow I remember a kind of rapport between them. I think they were talking when they came around the corner together."

"What's she saying?"

" 'I don't know my way around this part of the building.' She's saying something to me."

"Something to that effect? What happens now?"

"She comes . . . I don't think she presses the button because I'm standing almost in front of her. She'd have to reach in front of me. She sees it has already been pressed."

"Is there only one elevator there, Laura?"

"Yes."

"I see. What happens now?"

"She asks me if I'm performing tonight. I said that I had performed. . . . She says, 'I have to speak with Mr. Panov.' She asks if Mr. Panov is busy now, if it's a good time to talk to him. And she's carrying something."

"She's carrying something? How is she holding it?"

"She could be holding it to her chest, loosely, like a book or something. And I say it's probably fine now. He's had some time to rest up and probably wouldn't mind."

"Where is the man?"

"He's to her left. He's not ignoring us."

"I want you to look at that man, Laura. And as you look at him, I want you to let time stand still. You stop moving, the woman stops moving, the man stops. Everything in the opera house stops moving. Time is standing still. This man and this woman are standing in front of you, as though they're in a portrait. Look at that man now and tell me about him."

"Hm. . . . He isn't well dressed. He's not wearing a suit."

"What color is his skin?"

"He's white."

"How tall do you think he is?"

"He could be a bit taller than me. I'm five foot seven and he's maybe five foot ten or so."

"Now suppose you just start with his hair and go down and tell me about him."

"He has fly-away hair. In any case, it isn't light blond. I think it's dark, probably dark brown, not very thick, not wavy or kinky, kind of sparse, not balding, but sparse."

"What length?"

"Not very long. Not like a hippie but also not terribly short. It's not very carefully arranged but it isn't, you know, especially sloppy. Maybe it covers part of his ears, but not terribly long. It could be parted and hanging partially onto his face."

"What else can you tell me about him?"

"I don't think he has a beard but he could have. He might not be freshly shaven, and it's possible he has a mustache."

"Tell me about his features."

"He has a large face."

"Tell me about his eyebrows."

"They're dark."

"How would you describe them—as thin, thick, bushy?"

"They're not very thin."

"And what kind of eyes does he have?"

"They could be brown. They're not very large."

"Do you see the color?"

"They're brown. Could be blue."

"Brown or blue?"

"He's wearing blue."

"Oh, I see. How is he dressed?"

"Well, I have an impression of work clothes . . . fairly dark color. I think at the time I just assumed he was one of the technical men who work in the theater. I mean around the stage—lighting men and prop men and all the different jobs they have. I just sort of assumed he was one of these."

"Keep seeing him in the present tense. Would you describe him as a good-looking guy or what?"

"Not terribly. He isn't thin. He seems, I think, a bit overweight but not obese."

"How would you describe the way he looks? Would you say he's a pleasant fellow? Does he seem mean or kind?"

"He seems businesslike. He seems as if he has something to do. He's not hurried but he's going directly to get something done."

"Can you see him clearly now?"

"No."

"You don't see him clearly? Perhaps as we go along, there'll be a particular place where you see him more clearly than you do now—maybe a few seconds from now or in the elevator. So let's move along and let time start up again. You said this woman asks you if you were performing tonight and if this is a good time to see Mr. Panov. While you stand there, the elevator comes. What happens now? Tell me, Laura, when the time comes when you see this man more clearly than you did a few seconds ago. Let time stop again and just have him there. Look at him and tell me more about him. Okay, you tell me the story now. The elevator stops, the door opens. What happens now?"

"I'm telling her he's finished dancing. She says she doesn't want to bother him. It should be all right to go to him. . . . I thought this might be a good time. And I'm thinking, you know, who is this woman? Is she a ballet groupie who wants to come see the stars? Or perhaps she's a journalist because of the way she said, you know, I'm supposed to speak with him."

"Is the elevator moving now, Laura?"

"No."

"Not yet? Okay. Have the doors closed yet?"

"No. We're inside. They're going to. I press the lower level C."

"I see. Now what happens?"

"She's in the middle of the elevator. I'm toward the front on her left side. He's toward the front on the right side. She doesn't know where to find Panov. 'Where is his dressing room? Where would I find him?' The man says the third floor. She looks at him. He seems confident about the third floor. If he hadn't said that, it would've occurred to me that the soloists all have their dressing rooms on the stage level. I would've thought that Panov's dressing room was around from where they had been walking. But because the man said that right away, I didn't think about it, and I haven't been to Panov's dressing room. I just sort of . . . You know, we didn't know the opera house that well and he knows his way around. He can show her where to go to find Panov."

"Are you looking at this guy? Do you see him more clearly now than when you were standing in front of the elevator?"

"Yes."

"And the man has pressed number three?"

"Yes."

"Okay. What happens now?"

"She repeats that she knows how busy Panov is. And she asks me if Mr. Panov speaks English. I say yes, it's not so good but he speaks it. Then the elevator opens. She moves toward the back of the elevator as I get off. . . . He could be wearing boots. High, leather maybe."

"What color?"

"Brown."

"Does he have anything with him, Laura? Is he carrying anything or wearing anything?"

"No . . . a pocket on his chest, maybe . . ."

"Maybe what, Laura?"

She searched her mind for the answer but it didn't come.

"Does the clothing this man is wearing appear to be some kind of uniform?"

"Not so much a uniform . . ."

"Does what he's wearing have any writing or emblems on it anywhere?"

"I don't think so."

"Okay, fine. Now listen to me carefully. In a moment I'm going to count to three. When I do, I'm going to press on your left shoulder and this will help put you deeper into relaxation and will enable you to see things even more clearly and more distinctly. Now, one, two, three, way down, way down. That's fine. What I'd like you to do now, Laura, is go back in your mind again and start over from the point where you come to the front of the elevator. You push the down button and you're standing there all by yourself. I want you to go over it in your mind silently. You don't have to tell me about it until you get to the point where you see this man more clearly than at any other time. When you see him more clearly, raise this finger for me so that I know what you're looking at."

I touched Laura's right index finger.

"Go ahead now. See yourself standing in front of the elevator. You push the button. You're standing there all alone. You're viewing this in your mind."

"Shall I tell you?"

"Yes, when you see him more clearly just raise this finger for me."

"I can't see him."

"I don't think you understand what I mean. There has to be some time when he's standing in front of the elevator with you or when he's on the elevator that you see him more clearly than at any other time. When you reach that particular point, I want you to raise your finger for me, okay? Start again now. You're standing in front of the elevator by yourself. When you reach that point, when you see him more clearly than at any other time, just raise your finger."

I waited a few moments. Sure enough, Laura's finger went up.

"Okay, fine. Lock that picture in your mind, Laura. Lock the memory of this fellow you see on Wednesday, July 23, in the opera house with Helen. In a moment I'm going to place my hand on your head. When I do this, it'll enable you to use your mind in a new and powerful way. It"ll enable you to see this person even more clearly. Just watch him closely."

I touched the top of Laura's head with my right hand.

"Lock the image of this man into your mind so that if you ever see him again or see a photo of him, you'll recognize him. Now describe him for me again."

"His hair is dark. It's parted on the wrong side of his head. . . ."

"Does he have any jewelry on?"

"No."

"Listen carefully when he walks onto the elevator. Do you hear any jingling?"

"No."

"Okay, I forgot to ask you before about his nose. How would you describe it?"

"It's not finely shaped. It's fairly big."

"And what about his lips?"

"His lips are bright red."

"Bright red?"

"Very."

"Is that a natural color?"

"Yes, as if he had been biting them."

"Are they thick or thin? What would you say?"

"His eyebrows?"

"No, I mean his mouth. How would you describe the size of his mouth?"

"It's not very big. There's hair around . . . black hairs, as if he didn't shave. . . ."

"Does he have sideburns?"

"Yes."

"Does he have any facial hair?"

"He has a mustache."

"Describe it for me."

"It's not very full. Dark brown."

"How wide is it?"

"About as wide as his lips."

"Is it straight or handlebar or curved down or anything like that?"

"It's straight."

"Okay, fine."

"It's not perfectly straight."

"I see. Does he have any lines on his face? What about his complexion?"

"It's all right. Not very tan."

"Any blemishes or marks of any kind?"

"No. . . . He had wrinkles in his forehead."

"I see, just normal wrinkles on the forehead?"

"Yes."

"How about his ears?"

"His ears are not very big. They don't show much. They're partially covered by his hair."

"How old do you think he is?"

"I think he's probably twenty."

"How old?"

"Twenty, twenty-five. I'm not sure."

"As you look at his clothing, can you tell me if his pants and shirt match? Are the shirt and trousers the same color?"

"Not exactly the same."

"How are they different?"

"The shirt is a bit lighter than the pants."

"Can you tell me about the material?"

"It's cotton or wool or something like that. It's not polyester. . . ."

"If you saw the material again, would you be able to identify it? In other words, if we showed you cotton or wool, would you be able to differentiate which one it was?"

"Yes."

"Okay, fine. You told me earlier that his shirt is open at the collar."

"Yes."

"Is he a hairy person?"

"Not terribly."

"Can you see hair on his chest where his collar is open?"

"Sometimes."

Laura was speaking so softly, I was sure the tape wasn't picking her up. "Could you just speak up a little, Laura, so we can get this on tape?"

"Yes."

"Good. That's better. Does he appear to be one of the security people to you?"

"No."

"If you had to take a guess about what he does, if he's employed here, what would you say? I know that's difficult, but just a guess."

"Don't know."

"What can you tell me about this fellow's voice when he speaks?"

"I know it doesn't especially strike me, so I guess it isn't terribly high or terribly low."

"Does he speak like an American?"

"Yes, he could be from New York. I don't notice any sort of accent that would be unusual—foreign or European."

"Do you notice when he talks to Helen about Panov's dressing room whether he smiles or anything?"

"I think he probably does because we're all being very friendly. I'm feeling . . . I know I remember that I was feeling elated because I had been inspired by something on the stage and I was going to go downstairs and work this out. And she came up and she seemed so happy. I'm sort of thinking to myself about this, that Panov has his fans. They're coming to see him. That was kind of funny to think about, and he was in the spirit as well. I think he probably did smile. He was being very friendly."

"Okay, fine. Now his hair. As I recall, you told me about it a few moments ago. You said it wasn't too thick. Can you explain what you mean by that?"

"I mean it's spread out . . . just not that thick."

More than likely at this point, Laura's subconscious had surrendered as complete a picture of the suspect as it contained. It didn't take much to see that the senseless killing weighed heavily on her mind, and there was no sense in adding further to the strain. I asked the two investigators if they would like to question the witness but both were satisfied with what we had. I released her from her trance, expressed our appreciation, and told her if she came up with anything more in the next day or two, to be sure to contact Detective Giorgio.

I had the distinct feeling that the barely audible responses Laura gave under hypnosis betrayed her reluctance to be instrumental in the identification of a suspected murderer. Like too many potential witnesses for the prosecution in this age of criminal leniency, Laura no doubt was afraid of retribution. Every possible means of ensuring her safety was seen to and the existence of her hypnotic testimony was kept under wraps until weeks later when a suspect was in custody. Ironically, when the investigators listened to a playback of the tape, Laura's voice was so weak that much of what she had to say couldn't be understood. Only after the tape had been sent to an audio lab and the sound enhanced, were the detectives able to hear her voice and re-examine her testimony. It was then they realized that, under hypnosis, Laura had judged the suspect's age to be twenty to twenty-five. At all other times, she said she thought he was in his late thirties.

Reluctant or not, Laura had given the investigators exactly what they were after—a glimpse of that man in the elevator. The dancer's clear hypnotic image of the suspect was recorded by a sketch artist soon after she had undergone my interrogation. The composite that emerged, plus some uncorroborated alibis, narrowed the field to three or four contenders. It was a short haul from that point in the case to a final arrest. A set of fingerprints had been found on the Met's sixth floor near a pile of Helen's clothes. Her hands had been bound with her own brassiere tied in a clove knot, customarily used by stagehands. On the basis of this information, along with a missed 9:50 P.M. cue, whereabouts unaccounted for, plus an eventual confession, twenty-one-year-old stagehand Craig Stephen Crimmins was charged with the murder of Helen Hagnes Mintiks.

Employed at the Met for four years, the Bronx resident was a high school dropout with a juvenile-arrest record. How closely did he resemble the composite drawn from Laura's description was the question I asked myself shortly after his incarceration. At first glance, the dissimilarities were very much apparent. The face in the rendering appeared to be older and scruffier-looking than the youthful stagehand's. No doubt the sketch artist took his cue from Laura's impression of the man as a worker with a day or two of stubble. Composite drawing is a highly subjective art. The finished product represents one individual's interpretation, and each sketch bears the personal stamp of the artist who executed it. My assistant, Millie, maintains she can always tell, by the general character and style of a composite, who among our staff artists drew it.

At any rate, on closer inspection, the sketch of the Phantom of the Opera—as we had taken to calling Miss Hagnes' murderer—

revealed strong resemblances to some of Crimmins' facial characteristics, particularly in the area of the mouth, mustache, and nose, and the way they related to each other. And the eyes, in my estimation, were those of the suspect, without a doubt.

In pretrial hearings, some months following Crimmins' arrest, Acting Justice Richard G. Danzer ruled the suspect's videotaped confession to the police admissible as evidence. Claiming that Miss Cutler's memory had been confused by suggestions made to her while under hypnosis, Crimmins' attorneys demanded that the ballerina's testimony be excluded from the trial. They pointed out that what she initially had told the police differed considerably from what she had said during the hypnotic interview. But Justice Danzer denied the request with the ruling, "the circumstances of the interrogation were such that no great risk of inaccuracy in the trial testimony was involved." The court's willingness to be open-minded in this instance, in the face of the usual criticisms and forebodings, was an encouraging sign that forensic hypnosis was gaining acceptance as a legitimate source of evidence for the prosecution.

The opera-company employee's trial for murder and attempted rape began on April 27, 1981, in Manhattan's state supreme court. On the fourth day of the proceedings, Laura Cutler was on the witness stand for three solid hours, subjected to grueling cross-examination by defense attorney Lawrence Hochheiser. After the dancer had been unable to certify that the defendant in the courtroom was the man she had described as being with Miss Hagnes in the backstage elevator nearly a year before, Mr. Hochheiser referred to the lineup Laura had viewed the previous September.

"Did you see that person in the lineup?" he asked.

"I don't know."

"Have you ever seen that person again?"

"I don't know."

"Did you look at the sketch after the sketch was completed?"

"Yes, I did."

"Did you tell the policemen that, according to your recollections, that was what the man looked like?"

"No, I didn't tell them that."

"Did you see the sketch after it was completed?"

"Yes, I did."

"Did it appear to be the man who was in the elevator?"

"I don't know. What I told them was that I didn't know what the man in the elevator looked like. I could remember very vaguely some things, and I don't know."

The incisive attorney discredited the star witness' testimony with calculated dispatch. But no matter. The evidence most damaging to the defense's case was the accused's confession. His attorneys contended that their client had been coerced by the police into making the incriminating admission, but the members of the jury didn't buy that. On June 4, 1981, after having heard five weeks of testimony, they found the defendant guilty.

On September 2, Judge Danzer sentenced the young man to imprisonment for twenty years to life for second-degree murder, recommending that he not be eligible for parole without having been confined for at least twenty years. As the prisoner listened impassively, the justice condemned his ignominious offense as "a cruel, brutal and barbaric crime."

6

A TECHNIQUE DEVISED

One of the reasons hypnosis is endlessly fascinating to me is that it deals directly with human nature in all its diversity. Much of the challenge that keeps my professional juices flowing would be gone if every hypnotic induction were a grounder, to borrow a baseball term that is also police jargon for a case that all but solves itself.

No two people are susceptible to hypnosis in exactly the same way. Every situation is unique. It is one thing to give a demonstration of hypnosis in a setting that allows a choice of subjects from a large group of people. It is quite another to have to deal with whoever comes in the door, even if he is the worst subject in the world. While I favor certain induction and deepening procedures to a degree because they have a good track record over a wide range of susceptibility, I know that every now and then I will run across an individual who will prove to be the exception.

During formal training at some of the best institutions in the country, I have learned a variety of methods for inducing hypnosis and encouraging deeper states. I have also accumulated a library of books on the subject, and I don't think I could find among them a single one I haven't learned something from. Even in the worst, there has been at least one small idea or technique I have turned around and adapted to my particular brand of hypnosis. This also applies to hypnotists. I like to watch over the shoulders of colleagues as often as possible. A few have whipped up some farfetched theories and put into practice a variety of outlandish procedures, but I know even those practitioners with the most questionable technique will show me something new and useful.

The one source that has given me more induction and deepening savvy than any other is on-the-job experience. Some of the witnesses and victims I have encountered have been such tough hypnotic subjects I have practically had to go through my whole repertoire of exercises before arriving at the one that produced results. To overcome unusual circumstances in a few instances, it has been necessary, at best, merely to modify an otherwise tried-and-true procedure and, at worst, to improvise a new one on the spot.

Four years ago I worked on an arson investigation. The fire destroyed a building that housed a neighborhood social club in Brooklyn and killed no less than twenty-five people. More than a hundred were gathered at the club for a dance when the flames hit. I hypnotized one of the survivors, an athletic young man named Raul Martinez, and it was no easy task. Like many of the others who had survived the blaze, Raul had saved himself by jumping from one of the club's second-story windows. His two sisters had not been as fortunate. The flames took their lives.

Evidence amid the ashes showed that somebody had set the fire deliberately. In the search for information leading to the perpetrator, the detective on the case looked to the people who had been at the dance. When questioned, Raul told him about an argument he had witnessed at the club. He had overheard a man asking the woman he was with to come home with him. The woman refused and the man slapped her. Then he started to leave, but before he got to the door, he turned to the woman and said, "You're gonna see what's gonna happen."

The investigator thought hypnosis might help Raul come up with a good description of the guy who had made the threat.

As a hypnosis subject, Raul was a real challenge. He didn't go under easily and when he did, he was in a very light state. Despite the difficulty, I did finally help him remember a minor detail that turned out to be the lead that cracked the case.

Raul's interview and that of the second case in this chapter offer a rich sampling of the special techniques I bring into play to release resistant memories and to deepen the trances of difficult subjects.

I started Raul's interview off with a standard induction. The young man was sitting comfortably in a chair in my office, and I had made sure he was as relaxed as possible before I began.

"All right, Raul," I said, "I want you to pick out any spot you like high up on the wall here and just gaze at it in an easy and effortless manner. Don't think about anything special. Just listen to me as you look at the spot. In a moment, I'm going to count to twenty very slowly. When I say 'one,' close your eyes and open them again. Keep looking at the spot. When I say 'two,' do the same thing, and so on with each count. As you do that and I continue to talk to you, you'll find that you'll begin to relax more and more. All your muscles will let go. Your breathing will become deeper, more regular, and with each count, your eyelids will become heavier and heavier. By the time I reach twenty, or maybe even before then, your eyelids will be so heavy, so sleepy you'll just want to leave them closed. When that happens, let them stay closed and drop right down into a deep, sound, relaxed hypnotic state."

I began the count and Raul closed and opened his eyes as I had asked him to. After each number, I coaxed him along with words of encouragement: "You're beginning to relax now. Your breathing is becoming deeper and more regular. . . . A pleasant heaviness, a strange dullness is starting to come over you. Your eyelids are beginning to feel like lead. . . . Every word I say relaxes you more and more. . . . Every time you inhale, you breathe in confidence and composure and relaxation. Every time you exhale, you breathe out tension and fear."

We got to the end of the count and Raul was only in a very light trance, if hypnotized at all. His eyes kept flickering open and he was fidgeting. I decided to go immediately into a deepening process.

I used a standard method, counting backward from ten to one with the word, deeper, between each count. That did the trick somewhat. Raul was responding, but I figured one more deepening technique was in order as a clincher.

"You're doing fine, Raul," I said. "The only thing important to you now is the sound of my voice, which is pleasing to your ears. Every word I say keeps sending you deeper and deeper into relaxation. The next thing I'm going to do is pick up your left hand. When I do that, you'll notice how loose and limp your whole arm is, just like a wet dish rag. On the count of three, I'm going to let go of your hand. Your arm will drop back down and you'll immediately go into an even deeper state than you're in now.

"Okay, here we go." I picked up Raul's hand. His arm was very limp, a good sign. "That's fine, Raul. Feel that relaxation. One, your arm is getting heavier and heavier. Two, heavier still, and three, all the way down now, way down, deep, deep asleep. That's fine. You're doing very well."

I was sure now that Raul was in a hypnotic state, albeit a light one. Before hitting him with questions about the fire, which had taken place two months prior to the interview, I thought it would be a good idea to stimulate his memory banks a little with a technique designed for that purpose.

"You'll find that it's very easy to recall certain things," I assured him, "in this state that you're in. For instance, I'd like you to go back in your mind to July of this year when you had a birthday. Try to remember the events of your last birthday, which I believe was on July 10. Is that right?"

Raul nodded an affirmative.

"Good. Now I'm going to tell you about something that'll help you go back in time. I want you to picture in your mind a large clock, the kind you find in schools, with big hands and numbers. But the strange thing about this clock is it runs backward. Try to see the hands on that clock going around backward faster and faster. Every time they go around once, another day goes by. When I say stop, the hands will stand still and it'll be July 10, 1977, the day of your birthday.

"Okay, see the clock running backward in time." I waited long enough for Raul to really get those hands going in his mind, and then called out, "Stop! Now tell me as much as you can about your birthday. You'll find, Raul, that you can speak easily and comfortably while under hypnosis. As a matter of fact, the act of speaking actually helps send you deeper and deeper into relaxation."

I asked Raul to tell me what he did on his birthday. Did he get any presents? What were they? He told me about a party at his house, the friends who were there, and the gifts they gave him. His memories of the day were rich in detail. They were percolating to the surface nicely, and he was ready now to take on the incidents we were concerned about.

I returned to the imagery of the backward-running clock to help Raul get a fix on the date of the fire: "Stop the clock! It's August 5, 1977, a day you'll never forget, a date that's so important to you that you can't help but remember everything that happened on it. You, your sisters Rita and Dolores, and a lot of people you know are going to the dance at the social club. Tell me what you did when you got to the dance."

Raul told about paying at the door to get in, going to the bar to buy himself and his sisters a beer, and then going back downstairs with his sisters to smoke a joint. When they finished the joint, they went upstairs again. Raul danced with one of his sisters. The music stopped and they sat down. That's when the argument broke out, the one Raul had already told the police about.

"Fifteen minutes after this guy leaves," Raul continued, "a lady yells, 'Fire!' We all look to the door. It's covered with flames. Everybody's screaming and jumping up and down. I tried to help a guy whose shirt caught on fire but I couldn't. He kept running around like he was crazy. My hair caught on fire. I put it out and then I fell on the floor."

"You fell on the floor?"

"Yeah, this guy ran into me and almost knocked me out. I

tried to help my sisters but I couldn't. The smoke was getting to me and I started feeling dizzy, losing my power. So I just jumped."

I asked Raul to describe the man who was involved in the argument. He told me what he was wearing but couldn't remember anything about his face. I could tell that a touch of anxiety was creeping in and getting in the way of Raul's relaxation. I wondered how deeply affected he was by the loss of his sisters and his own brush with death. I was more determined than ever to rid his mind of fear and anxiety by helping him experience the deepest hypnotic state he was capable of. It was time for another little exercise.

"In a moment I'm going to put my hands on your shoulders, Raul, and I'm going to count to ten. As I count, you'll go deeper and deeper. When I reach the count of ten, I'm going to push down on your shoulders and this will send you even deeper into hypnosis."

The technique worked well. Raul was once again calmer, more relaxed. I had a hunch he might be able to give us a description of the likely suspect if I brought him back to the beginning of the evening and then eased him into a confrontation with the man.

"I'm going to take you back to when you got to the club, Raul. This time, don't just tell us about what you remember but really try to relive things in your mind as they're happening. See the people dancing. Hear the music. Sense the excitement in the air, the smells. What time is it when you arrive at the dance?"

"About eleven forty-five. My friend Carlos drove us there."

"Who was that?"

"His name is Carlos."

"Did Carlos go to the dance with you?"

"No."

"He dropped you and your sisters off?"

"Yes."

This was a new name to add to the investigation. Raul hadn't mentioned anything about Carlos in his earlier statements to the detectives.

We plowed through the events of the evening step-by-step once more, but Raul still couldn't quite make out the face of the man we wanted him to tell us about. I knew he had seen more than a glimpse of this man. Under those circumstances, zeroing in on physical characteristics is normally no problem for hypnosis. I wasn't going to give up yet.

Bringing subjects out of hypnosis and then rehypnotizing them is a process that sometimes succeeds when all else fails. This is exactly what I did at this point with Raul. I returned him to full consciousness and as I prepared to put him under again, I assured him, "Now that you know the type of feeling we're looking for, you'll be able to tune in to it again very quickly. You'll have no trouble going right into an even deeper state than you were in before."

We used the spot-on-the-wall induction once more. It put Raul into a nice, solid trance. To coax him to let go to his fullest capacity, I selected a deepening technique we hadn't tried yet.

"In this condition you're in now, Raul, many people have the ability to visualize a scene much more vividly than they can in what we call the waking state. I'm going to set up a scene for you now and I'd like you to picture it in your mind.

"I want you to see yourself standing at the top of an escalator that's moving down slowly away from you. In a moment I'm going to ask you to see yourself stepping onto that escalator and going down. The escalator seems to have ten steps, and on the wall going down alongside it, are large numbers. Do you see the number ten right next to you?"

Raul nodded.

"And down a little further you see the number nine, and then the number eight, and so on. When you step onto the escalator, it'll take you down one step at a time. With every step, you'll go deeper into hypnosis, so that when you reach the bottom, the next floor down, you'll be in the deepest state you've ever been in and ready to receive the important instructions I'm going to give you."

I guided Raul down the escalator, encouraging him to go deeper and deeper as he glided past one number and then another. When we got to the bottom, I said, "As you step off the escalator, Raul, you seem to be in a grassy area. You can feel the soft grass underneath your feet, and all around you is a garden. Some of your favorite flowers are growing in this garden, and you can smell them. Birds are singing in the trees and nearby a brook is gurgling. You look ahead of you and see a bench. Walk over to the bench and sit down. As you sit there in this beautiful garden, you go into the deepest, most profound state of hypnosis you've ever experienced. Good. That's it, go deeper . . . deeper.

"I'd like to ask you a few questions now. You can answer these questions easily just by raising a finger. If you want to answer yes, you can raise your right index finger. For no, just raise your left index finger, okay?

"Were you able to see the numbers on the side of the escalator?"

Raul raised his right index finger.

"Fine. And could you feel the grassy area when you stepped off?"

The right finger went up again.

"That's good."

I asked about the flowers and bench. Raul's right-hand finger popped up in response to both. I was beginning to feel more optimistic. Maybe we would get the description we wanted after all.

"You've visualized this scene so well, Raul, that I'm going to ask you to picture something else. I want you to forget about the garden and see yourself safe and secure in your own bedroom at home. You're lying in bed and you've just turned the television on. In a moment the set will light up and you'll see a documentary film about the fire at the club. You'll be in complete control of the film. You can speed it up, slow it down, zoom in for close-ups of things you can't see too clearly. You'll even be able to reverse the film and view it over and over if you want to. All the while, you'll remain calm and composed, and if at any time you want to stop the film, just reach over and turn the set off, okay?

"The film is coming on now, the screen is lighting up, and you're beginning to see a documentary that shows exactly what took place on the night of August 5. Tell us what's happening on the screen."

"I can't see it."

"That's okay, Raul. Don't worry about it. You're doing fine. You have to go a little deeper before you can actually do it. Just go back in your mind now to that night at the club. Try to picture the room where the dance was held as clearly as you saw the garden. See the man and woman arguing. They're only five feet away from you. You say his face was turned away slightly, but he certainly didn't stay in that position all the time he was there. I'm sure he moved around, maybe danced. You must have gotten a good look at him at some point. Visualize that face and describe it to us."

Raul frowned and shook his head from side to side.

"You can't do it? Okay, Raul, if you didn't see it, then it's just impossible for you to do it, right?"

I had reached the end of the line. There were no more tricks up my sleeve. I was resigned to the fact that if Raul had any memory at all of that face, it would have surfaced by now. As a last-ditch effort, I turned to Detective John McGrath, who had been working with me at the time, and asked him to give it a try.

Despite McGrath's hypnotic skill and a few tricks of his own, Raul still wasn't able to tell us anything about our mystery man. We brought the subject out of his trance and thanked him for his co-operation. We were disappointed. But what we didn't know then was that Raul and hypnosis had already given us the clue that would eventually wrap up the case for its investigator.

Under hypnosis, Raul had said that somebody named Carlos had driven him and his sisters to the club but didn't attend the dance. The detective decided to find this guy Carlos, thinking he might have some information that would prove helpful. It was a lucky break. On the basis of Carlos' statements and further evidence, he and a pyro friend of his were arrested on a charge of arson.

It turned out that Carlos was Raul's sister Rita's boyfriend. He had set the fire in a fit of jealousy over a boy who was a rival for Rita's affections. The rival had been at the dance with Rita, and Carlos was hell-bent on revenge.

One of the more ingenious techniques I tried with Raul, the television screen documentary, didn't work because the boy wasn't in a deep enough trance. Under the right conditions, this exercise is an excellent way to remove the subject from the fear and anxiety associated with re-experiencing the crime. It is as if he isn't involved at all, but watching someone else enact his part in the incident.

Dr. Herbert Spiegel, whom I studied with at the Columbia College of Physicians and Surgeons, taught me an interesting variation on the television screen theme. My adaptation of it for forensic purposes is a sure-fire means of recovering details that may have been recorded by the subconscious but are not available to the conscious memory. Its effectiveness, again, depends on how deeply hypnotized the subject is. Instead of one screen with one image, I have the witness envision a split screen. "On the right side of the screen," I tell him, "you'll see what you saw with your conscious mind. On the left, you'll see the same incident, but with details picked up by your subconscious." I ask the subject to tell me about any differences he sees between the two images. This often uncovers new information, things the witness is otherwise unconscious of.

A widely favored induction technique I haven't mentioned involves the use of what are known in the trade as hypnodiscs. These are circles of cardboard, about ten inches across, that are printed with spiral patterns. When the discs are spun on an upright turntable-like machine, their patterns appear to converge at the center like a whirlpool. An observer staring at the rotating design long enough begins to feel as if he were being drawn into it. Like pendulums and flashing lights, the discs serve as visual fixation points for lulling subjects into hypnosis.

Four hypnodiscs hang on one wall of my office. Aside from their decorative value, the familiar-looking patterns offer visitors the subliminal message that this is a place where hypnosis is practiced. I rarely use the discs for their intended purpose. I begin all interviews with the Hypnotic Induction Profile, and at the end of this procedure, the subjects' eyes are closed. It would be an unnecessary disturbance to have these people open their eyes and stare at a spinning disc. But hypnodiscs are a perfectly acceptable means of hypnosis and are widely used by respectable practitioners.

In the same year as the social club fire, my services were required on another case that demanded special handling. I was asked to interrogate an assault victim who happened to be the wife of a New York City policeman. The nature of the physical injury the woman had suffered as a result of the assault made it impossible to hypnotize her with any of my standard techniques. To make matters worse, just as I was preparing her for the escalator deepening process described in Raul Martinez's interview, I discovered she had a terrible fear of stairways, moving or not. Like a quick-change artist, I improvised a modification right on cue.

Early in the evening, on a balmy Saturday in October 1977, the sidewalks of Manhattan's East Side were alive with the usual throngs of obviously successful career people, outfitted in the latest studied-casual gear and rushing to complete weekend errands.

Like the others, Janet Nicholson had an air of self-assurance about her. She was an attractive woman of thirty-five and a hard-working divorce lawyer. The day away from her job hadn't dispelled the tension and exhaustion that had accumulated during an especially demanding week. Janet wondered how she was going to get through the next, as she left a midtown office-supply store with her purchases.

She made a deliberate effort to unwind while walking the few crosstown, tree-lined blocks that separated the store from her high-rise apartment building. She had started thinking about the strategy she was planning for one of her clients, but stopped herself abruptly. Instead, she focused her attention on the setting sun and the soft, pink light it cast on the leaves overhead. Her husband would be off-duty soon and Janet looked forward to the rare occasion of a Saturday night shared with him.

As she approached the building, she was reminded once more that it had no doorman. Except for the lack of this extra measure of security, Janet was happy with all aspects of her apartment and its location. She thought maybe she was being a bit paranoid. After all, the inside door of the entrance was always locked. Residents had to use their keys to get in and visitors had to be buzzed in through the intercom.

She pushed open the unlocked outer door and stepped into the building's vestibule. As she set her packages down, she became aware of another presence behind her. She turned her head to see who had come in the door and the next thing she knew, her face was splashed with a liquid of some kind.

"My God, what the hell is this?" Janet thought. She recoiled instinctively and almost hit her head against the glass door behind her. The intruder had disappeared. She realized to her horror that her face was beginning to feel as though it were on fire. The drops of liquid falling on her coat were burning holes through the fabric. She touched her finger tips to her face and they, too, started to feel hot.

Janet let out a terrorized shriek. She was heard by the building's superintendent, who came running.

"My face . . . my face," Janet gasped. "It must be acid or something," she cried out in pain. "It's burning my skin."

The super rushed her into the janitor's washroom, helped her bathe her face with water, and then ran off to call an ambulance.

When Janet had calmed down enough to think about it, she was grateful she had been wearing sunglasses when the acid hit. She was still able to see, but her eyes were burning and she was sure that some of the liquid had run into them before she was able to bathe her face.

Sergeant Mark Nicholson, one of New York's finest, was at his wife's bedside in Mount Sinai Hospital when Detective Marty Rollins arrived. Janet was under sedation. Her swollen eyes and the red, running sores on her face spoke eloquently of the assault she had suffered.

"Who did this to you, Janet?" Marty asked.

Despite the disorienting effect of the sedative, Janet tried to pull together her recollections of the incident. She remembered that her vision had been obscured the instant the acid hit her glasses. "But did I see the person before that, when I first turned around?" she asked herself. The image of a dark figure emerged.

"All I can say with any certainty," she replied to Marty, "is that it was a black man."

"Could it have been the husband of the black woman whose divorce you've been working on?" Marty asked.

"I just can't say for certain," Janet replied.

But as far as Marty was concerned, this man was the only logical perpetrator. "It's got to be the husband," he said to Sergeant Nicholson, "but I think it would be a good idea to take Janet down to the Hypnosis Unit and see if we can get a full description."

This MO is typical of many of the cases that make use of my services. An investigator reconstructs a sequence of events based on circumstances and sketchy evidence. Then he brings a witness or victim to me merely to verify what he feels he already knows. But the information derived through hypnosis often calls for an about-face.

Marty brought Janet to police headquarters directly from the hospital and would be returning her there immediately after the interrogation. The lesions on her face were running profusely and had to be dabbed at constantly. I knew this was going to be a difficult session. I tried to make Janet as comfortable as possible, and then wondered how I was going to hypnotize her.

Ordinarily I use the eye-roll induction or I say to a subject, "Close and open your eyes very slowly. Every time you do that, your eyes will become heavier and heavier, and soon they'll be so heavy you won't be able to open them."

But Janet's eyes were tearing and swollen almost completely shut, so this approach was impossible. Instead, I decided to have her imagine she was in a soothing, restful setting. I said to her, "Picture yourself lying on the most beautiful beach you've ever seen. The ocean breezes are gently caressing your skin and you feel more relaxed and contented than you've ever felt in your life."

It took some doing to get Janet to really fix on this image but I kept at it. When I eventually succeeded in getting her into a light hypnotic state, I said to her, "Now you're going to get up and take a walk to the edge of the water. Let the rolling surf lap at your feet. It'll make you feel good all over. Look down into the water. You'll begin seeing the image of a man, faintly at first and then more and more clearly. Can you see that image?"

"Yes I can," Janet replied in almost a whisper.

"Good," I reassured her. "The man you're seeing is the man who attacked you, and now you should be able to tell us exactly what he looks like. Can you do that?"

"Not really," she replied. "It just isn't clear enough."

I decided we needed a break. I was relieved that my induction attempt had succeeded but I didn't want to push Janet too far. I was sure I could get her to confront her assailant after she had rested for a few minutes.

As soon as I brought her out of the trance, she said, "One thing I'm positive about now is it's *not* my client's husband. I can't see the image clearly enough to give you a description but it definitely doesn't look like Maria's husband Victor."

Marty thought he had the case all wrapped up, so this came as a big surprise. "Okay, if it wasn't him, then what did this person look like?" he said with annoyance.

I eased Janet back into a trance and told her, "Now don't think about your assailant for a moment. I want you just to go back in your mind to that evening. And at the same time, I want you to realize that you're here with us, that nothing can happen to you. Just remain in this deep, relaxed state. Keep your eyes closed. Keep breathing deeply. Keep relaxing more and more. In this calm state, it's going to be very easy for you to recapture the thoughts that proved so difficult to remember while fully conscious.

"Do you have packages with you when you arrive at the apartment?"

"I had two or three shopping bags."

"Can you remember some of the things you bought?"

"Yes, a box of Manila folders for my office and a typewriter cover. I tried to get a ribbon but they didn't have the right one."

"That's very good. What's the weather like?"

"It was moderate. I had a coat on, but a light jacket would've been enough."

"How are you feeling as you walk home?"

"Well, I had a lot of work to do." Janet chuckled. She was getting more relaxed. "I guess I was thinking how I would cope with it all."

"And you walk into the lobby of your building?"

"Well, you can't walk in because the lobby is behind locked doors. I walked into this tiny little . . ."

"Entryway?"

"Yes, almost at street level."

"Uh-huh."

"It's just above street level."

"Do you need a key to open the doors to the lobby?"

"Yes, the inner doors are supposed to be locked."

"Were they locked that day?"

"I think they were. They probably were. I don't know. . . . I didn't have time to find out."

"Do you have your key out as you approach the door?"

Janet was breathing heavily. "It was a little complicated, but I . . . I think what happened was that I was going to get my key out. But I sensed without seeing him that there was someone else there with me. And I don't know why . . . maybe I wasn't sure if he was another tenant or not, or maybe I felt somehow he wasn't. . . ."

"Uh-huh."

"But I didn't want to let myself in with him there. So . . . Isn't it stupid what women do? I mean, we're just too polite. I didn't want to look at him and walk away or, I don't know, start screaming. I'd never feel there was a reason to do that, just looking at someone. But I pretended I wasn't going to get my key out. I was going to ring the bell and wait for someone to let me in. I wanted to give him time to get his key first and see if he really lived there. It's very mixed up because I thought Mark wasn't home yet, you know? He was by a few minutes but I didn't know that. Anyway, I decided to try our bell and I was just reaching for it . . ."

"Okay, I want you to back up a bit now. I'd like you to think about walking toward your apartment door. See yourself walking along the street. Do you see anybody on the street? Are there people walking back and forth?"

"There isn't a whole crowd of people. Uh . . . I have a vague memory that . . . maybe one person behind me and another in front of me."

"Do you notice anybody who appears to be suspicious in any way, or out of place?"

"No, not really. I tend to walk along in a trance sometimes."

"Okay, how about automobiles? Is there a lot of parking around your . . . ?"

"There is a lot of parking and it's usually . . . Well, you can't find a legal place to park and there's a lot of double-parking."

"I see. So there's nothing that catches your eye . . . nothing unusual?"

"I did have a vague feeling that there were two cars double-parked right in front of our apartment and that they were dark and . . ."

"Dark in color?"

"Uh-huh. They may have been. They weren't, like, super new cars, but . . ."

"Is anybody in them?"

"I'm really uncertain of this, but my impression is that there was no one in them."

"Okay."

"But somehow . . . I don't know if I just imagine this, but near the edge of the street as I'm coming home, I just seem to sense a black man."

"Where?"

"I don't know if I'm being realistic . . . like, maybe standing by a car or something."

"Okay, just go over it in your mind. Just relax. Take a nice deep breath and let it out slowly. Relax even more and see yourself walking down the street. Try to pick up all the little feelings you have. Are you warm? Are you cold? Is the sun out? Is it cloudy? Let these things filter through your mind."

"I guess I'm more certain that there were probably one or two kids . . ."

"Uh-huh. Now continue. You're walking along the street. Are you walking fast or slow? How would you describe it?"

"I was walking sort of fast. I had these heavy packages."

I paused for a moment and looked at Janet. I searched her face for signs of tension. Before we got to the crucial confrontation, I wanted to make sure her calm recollections wouldn't be blocked by any feelings of fear or anxiety.

"Okay now," I said to her, "it's important that you just sort of let this thing happen by itself. Don't try to force anything. Any time you feel you're getting a little worked up or nervous, just take a very deep breath and let it out slowly. This will allow all your muscles to let go completely, as though they were pieces of wet rope, really slack."

"Uh-huh."

"What happens when you walk through the outside doors?"

"I don't think I had a . . . really suspicious feeling or anything. I just don't like it when I don't know the person coming in right behind me."

"Okay, good. Now stand there inside the doors and realize that someone is behind you. How do you . . . ?"

"Right, there's a male standing . . . I don't know why, but I sensed it was a male."

"How do you know there's someone behind you?"

"Oh, I'm absolutely certain of it."

"How do you know that? Do you hear someone walking?"

"I don't know if I heard him walking . . . or just heard him, like, being there."

"How do you feel?"

"I felt uneasy because it's a situation I don't like. And as a woman, I felt really vulnerable. I wasn't going to look at him and say, 'Do you live here?' or something like that."

"It's a Mexican standoff?"

"Well, I was with Mark once and he actually asked someone if they lived there. I've never done that and I don't know what I'd do if they seemed super suspicious or anything."

"Okay, Janet, I want you to put yourself in that hallway and I want you to talk in the present tense so we can make this more realistic for you."

"Uh-huh."

"As long as you can remain relaxed, you'll find that you'll have no problem going back over this thing in your mind. Don't say, 'I *was* there.' Say, 'I *am* there.' Now tell me what happens."

"I think I'm just reaching to ring my doorbell and I hear this really weird sound behind me."

"Does this person speak?"

"No, it's just a sound."

"Is it like someone clearing his throat?"

"I think . . . I don't know, maybe whistling. But I'm not going to look at this guy."

"All right, stop right there. You turn around and look."

"Yeah."

"What do you see?"

"I see sort of a flat, black male face. It's very hard to judge his age. He could be thirty. He could be younger. He could be older. I mean . . . maybe he's twenty-five to thirty-seven."

"Try to stop the action there and look at this fellow. Can you describe him to us? Do it piecemeal. Start with the top of his head."

"It's really freaky. I'm standing there, and for some reason, I'm really studying this man. It's like I don't have anything else to do but study his appearance. That's what I'm doing item by item. Well, okay, his hair. It's kinky, definitely kinky. It's not close-cropped but it's not an Afro either. It's maybe an inch and a half long. I'm getting this picture of a touch of white in his hair but I think I'm wrong. And then his face . . . it's real flat and it's an even color—closer to black than brown, sort of a dark chocolate. He's definitely not light-skinned. I'm really struck by what he's wearing. I don't know why."

"What's he wearing?"

"A gray tweed overcoat and it seems to me that it comes . . . it's very long, below the knee considerably. And I guess he might be a little younger than I first thought. I'm not sure."

"How old do you see him as?"

"Well, the figure that jumps into my mind is twenty-five but that may be too young. It's just hard to guess his age, but maybe he's not as far along toward thirty-seven as I thought when I saw him."

"Somewhere in the vicinity of twenty-five to thirty-five maybe?"

"Uh . . . that's my impression. It's not necessarily a logical impression but that's what was in my head that day."

"Let's go back to the overcoat for a moment. It's very long, you say?"

"Yes. And somehow I have the impression of a belt."

"Does the coat have buttons?"

"Yes."

"What kind of buttons?"

"Um . . . well, sort of gray plastic overcoat buttons."

"Large?"

"Medium, close to the size of a quarter."

"Okay, that's very good, Janet. What I'd like you to do now is to relax even more. You're not afraid of escalators are you?"

"I am, actually."

"You are?"

"Terribly."

"How about staircases?"

"Uh-huh."

"Elevators?"

"Uh . . . less so."

"Okay, I'd like you to imagine that you're standing in front of elevator doors. The doors open and you look inside. It's almost as if this is your private elevator because when you step into it, you notice wall-to-wall carpeting, lounge chairs, pictures on the walls. These pictures include some of your favorites. There's also a vase with some of your favorite flowers in it. You sit down in one of the more comfortable chairs and you look at the lights above the door. You notice that you're on the tenth floor. The doors close and you relax completely. The elevator starts down slowly and you sit there really enjoying the relaxation of this moment."

I waited for the imagery to take shape in Janet's mind before going on.

"The elevator goes down slowly to the ninth floor. You know you've arrived at the ninth floor because the number ten goes out and the number nine comes on. You really begin to relax. The elevator moves down again. It comes to the eighth floor. The number eight lights up and you're relaxing more. Now you're moving again and seven lights up. Once more down slowly and six lights up. You're really letting go. You're enjoying this private elevator ride a lot."

"It's a very unrealistic story," Janet laughed.

"Okay, you're a realistic person. That's fine. But try to enjoy it just the same. The main thing is to imagine it, to see it in your mind, to feel yourself floating down in this elevator.

"Now the elevator stops and the doors open. As you step off the elevator, you seem to be in a garden. Your feet sink into soft grass. All around you are trees, beautiful flowers, and birds are singing. Somewhere nearby a brook is running along. You walk over to a white bench and sit down. You float into a deep relaxation.

"Now I want you to go back. Remain in this deep, relaxed

state and go back to where you were standing. I want you to see this person in front of you. See him clearly in your mind's eye, just standing there. Can you see him now?"

"No, I don't."

"I just want you to see him in your mind's eye. The image may even develop to the point where you can see him as though he were on a television screen. But for the time being, I just want you to sort of remember what he looks like, to see him standing there."

"His eyes . . . I don't know, it's hard to express it. They weren't set very deeply into his face. And they're on the blue-gray side. That's the impression I get."

"You know they're not brown?"

"I don't know for sure. I just have an impression of blue or gray."

"How about facial hair?"

"None."

"No mustache?"

"No, I don't remember any facial hair at all."

"Have you ever seen this person before?"

"I don't think so."

"Okay, just relax now. I want you to take a couple of deep breaths and really let yourself go. In a moment I'm going to count to three and knock on the wall like this."

I struck the wall sharply with the knuckles of my hand.

"When you hear that sound, Janet, I don't want you to do anything. I just want you to become as relaxed as you can. Try to become a part of the chair."

"Can I tell you something about him first?"

"Sure."

"You know . . . I'm sure it wasn't Maria's husband because . . . maybe I'm not describing it very well, but it's like his chin doesn't curve out as much as the average person's does. It wasn't distorted or weird or anything. It's just that I get a strong impression that his face is unusually flat."

"Okay, let's see if we can do this now. Let yourself go. I want you to call out yes, you've seen this person or no, you haven't seen him before. I don't want you to think about it. Let the answer come spontaneously, all right? Now."

I hit the wall with my knuckles.

"I'm sorry but I can't stop seeing him. And I want to tell you what I see before I forget. I'm getting this image that he's maybe three inches taller than I am. But I can't remember how the steps in our vestibule are. I may have been standing one step above him. But I think he's taller than I am—at least average height and maybe a little taller than average."

"Let me see if I understand this now. If you were standing on this step, or whatever it was, he would probably be six or seven inches taller than you?"

"Yeah, that sounds like . . . five might be better, or around there."

"Anything else?"

"Let me think. He's got very ordinary hair, and his skin . . . I don't like to say rich because that's a favorable adjective, but deep, dark brown, sort of a smooth color. His face isn't broken. I mean it's just smooth skin and it's one shade. It's dark, maybe like Hershey's chocolate or a little darker. His fingers are roughly normal size and his hands may be a little younger than I thought."

"Any jewelry . . . rings?"

"I don't know. . . . I have a vague impression of a plain gold ring on one of his fingers."

"If you see this person again will you recognize him?"

"I think I would to some degree. I don't know if I'd recognize him as one of a group of ten people who looked similar, but then again maybe I would. I'm inclined to think that there was a small touch of white in his hair. There was nothing outstanding about the way he was dressed. He wasn't shabby and he wasn't all dolled up. He was just, you know, a black man."

"How close are you to him?"

"We were standing right next to each other."

"Can you smell anything?"

"No."

"Alcohol?"

"No."

"Shaving lotion?"

"No."

"Body odor?"

"No."

"I understand that you've met this fellow, Maria's husband . . ."

"Yeah. It's just my feeling after being through this that it wasn't Victor himself."

"As you were describing this fellow a few moments ago, you seemed to have a pretty good picture of him in your mind."

"Because I kept staring at him."

"If it is Victor, don't you think you'd be able to tell?"

"I don't know. I can't imagine what he'd look like without his beard."

"How long are you standing there before the assault takes place?"

"I guess a fraction of a minute . . . well, about twenty-five seconds."

"That long?"

"It seemed longer to me. It seemed like I was studying him in some timeless way. I remember now that I really did notice him. I mean, I did it consciously. I searched his face and I observed that overcoat, which just fascinated me. We just sort of stared at each other."

"Is anything said between you?"

"Not a word. Absolutely nothing."

"When do you realize that something is going to happen?"

"I don't know. It seems to me that logically I should have been thinking about rape or mugging except that we were so close to the street. But I don't know . . . if I was in fear, it was paralyzing me from seeing what was going to happen. I don't think I was expecting him to do something bad to me, although maybe somewhere in my head . . . It was more like I'm standing there in a strange situation and I'm studying this man and I'm noticing how long his overcoat is and how his eyeballs aren't set as far back in his head as most people's."

Janet was becoming agitated. Her eyes were tearing heavily and the sores on her face were oozing liquid. A break was definitely in order. Mark Nicholson gently dabbed at his wife's face with a tissue while he whispered words of encouragement. When Janet had regained her composure and was beginning to look relaxed again, I said to her, "You're really doing a great job for us here today and we appreciate it. Just bear with us a little longer and it'll all be over. Do you think you could try one more routine with me?"

"Yes. I'm fine. This is actually very interesting. It's a very interesting experience."

"Notice how the minor details come back, how they pop into your mind's eye. Now this next thing is up to you. You're the one who has to do it. You have to become really passive. Make yourself comfortable. Let all your muscles go and just become part of the furniture. Can you do that?"

"I'm sorry, I keep thinking of more things . . ."

"Good. That's great. As you think of them tell them to me."

"I keep seeing that flat face and I remember he had a broad forehead."

"Would you say he has begun to lose his hair?"

"No, definitely not, because the kinkiness, the first little curls, came right at the front where they normally would. His hairline wasn't receding."

"If you think of anything like that as we go along, just interrupt me and tell us. What seems to happen in these situations is we get the memory rolling. Little things come back and little things are connected to bigger things. No matter what we're doing, if there's anything you suddenly think of, make sure you bring it up so you won't forget it, okay?"

"I have the impression that his ears were like . . ."

"His ears are what, Janet?"

"His ears were normal to large size."

"Uh-huh."

"They didn't stand out from the sides of his head more than normal. If anything, the opposite. They were a little closer and a little more at right angles . . ."

"Is it still light out? I believe it's seven o'clock."

"I think it must have been a little earlier. Uh . . . it wasn't dark."

"Is the vestibule lighted?"

"Yes, I think there was a light on."

"Do you notice if he has an earring in his ear?"

"Oh, I'm absolutely certain of it. He didn't have an earring."

"Okay, Janet, I'm going to count backward very slowly from ten to one. I want you to repeat the numbers to yourself and relax more and more with each one. Stop me if you remember anything you haven't told us."

I finished the count. Janet hadn't stopped me, but she was now in a deeper trance.

"Just try to remain as passive as possible. When I knock on the wall, I want you to call out either, yes, or no. Answer without thinking about it in any way—yes, to indicate you've seen this person somewhere before, no, to indicate you've never seen him before. But I don't want you to think about it."

"Uh-huh."

"All right, one, two, three."

I knocked on the wall.

"No, I've never seen him before."

"You never saw him before? Are you sure?"

"Well, I'm not sure, but I never saw him before to know him. I mean, he's definitely not someone I ever met."

"You don't have to answer this next question if you don't want to. If you do see him again, would you be willing to say, 'Yes, this is the man'?"

"I would want to. I want to know who this character is."

"Good. Fine. Stay relaxed. You've told us about his ears and his eyes. Does anything strike you about his lips?"

"They were average black lips, which I guess means they were thick. But I'm not sure if they were really thick or just slightly thicker. . . . Wait a minute, maybe they're not as thick as I thought they were. And they're a little lighter in color than the rest of his face. I'm just seeing them now and I notice little lines in them that are darker than the rest of the lips."

"Would you regard him as a black person having medium-thick lips?"

"Yes, medium or somewhat less. But probably fuller than white."

"I see. Would you be willing to look at some pictures?"

"Oh, sure, sure. Hey, I just remembered that he was holding, like, a little pot with a black handle with the stuff in it."

"A pot?"

"Yeah. It was just an ordinary kitchen pot. It was, like, gray enamel and about four and a half or five inches across. It wasn't, like, a steel pot . . ."

"Does it have a handle?"

"Yeah, it had a small handle."

Marty Rollins interrupted: "Did she see where it came from?"

"That's a good question. Did you hear that, Janet?"

"No, I didn't."

"Detective Rollins was wondering where the pot came from. Is he hiding it?"

"I'm not sure . . . Oh, dear . . . Okay, he was holding it in his arm."

"In his right arm?"

"Yeah, I think so, but I don't think it was completely concealed. I don't remember if I noticed it right away. . . . I really hate this guy, naturally."

"Oh, of course."

"I'm very interested in knowing who he is. I have a feeling Maria's husband is involved with him somehow."

"You don't feel that when you turn around and finally look at this person, you see the pot immediately?"

"I'd doubt it. He was very smart. I mean, if you wanted to get someone to turn around, you'd make a sound just like he did."

"What kind of a sound?"

"I'm not sure. It was guttural, really weird."

"He does it with his vocal cords?"

"Yeah. . . . I don't know. . . . I mean, Victor was very freaky and he was capable of having friends who'd go around throwing acid at people. And he'd probably get a sexual kick out of it. He'd have friends who'd like to find out what it's like."

"If he did have someone do it."

"Oh, I have no doubt of that."

"Okay, Janet, you've done a great job and we really appreciate it. I just want to tell you that in the next night or two you may or may not have a dream regarding this incident. Is that all right with you?"

"Yeah."

"If you do have a dream, it may contain some new information that we haven't come up with. You'll be able to remember this dream and tell us about it, okay? Now I'm going to awaken you, which is a misnomer because you're not really asleep. But we don't have a better word to describe it. I'm going to count to five and on the count of five, your eyes will open. You'll be refreshed, relaxed, and rested. You'll feel better than you have in weeks.

"One, you're coming out of it feeling very, very good. Two, you're waking feeling refreshed, relaxed, and rested. Three, four, and five, you're wide awake and feeling fine."

"Oh!" Janet took a deep breath and exhaled slowly.

"Okay?"

"Yes, yes, fine. I feel wonderful."

"The time is 1315 hours and this is the end of the interrogation."

Janet was obviously relieved that the ordeal was over. She told me she had been very apprehensive at the thought of having to relive the incident under hypnosis. But to her amazement, she found that the hypnotic experience enabled her "to get it all off my chest. I feel a lot calmer and less distressed than I did before you hypnotized me."

Marty escorted Janet and Mark back to the hospital and then drove directly to Queens. He paid a call on Maria Alvarez, Janet's client.

"We thought your husband fit the bill to a tee," he told the young woman. "We were sure he was the one who sprayed Janet Nicholson. Now we're not so sure. We're looking for someone fitting a description Janet just gave us."

Marty told Maria about the flat facial features, long gray tweed coat, and touch of white in the hair.

"Oh my God," she exclaimed. "That sounds just like George! He's an old friend of my husband's."

The detective went looking for George and found him wearing a coat like the one Janet was so fascinated by. His physical characteristics fit Janet's description like a glove. Marty took him in and booked him on an assault charge. He also brought in Victor Alvarez, the man who put George up to the foul deed.

About a week after the assault, Marty arranged a lineup. He brought Janet down to headquarters and had her look at nine similar-appearing black men from behind the protection of a two-way mirror. One of the men was George. The suspect saw only a reflection of himself among the other men and heard nothing at the moment Janet said, "That's him, third from the right. I'm absolutely sure of it."

Some weeks after George and Victor had been arrested and released on bail, I was lecturing to a group of detectives in Westchester County. I happened to describe the investigation of the Janet Nicholson assault. When the lecture was over, the chief of police of Camden, New York, came up to me and said he had something to tell me about the case.

It seemed a woman had been driving down Camden's main street a few weeks back when her car was struck in the rear. As she got out to survey the damage, the driver of the other car, a man wearing a stocking mask, got out, ran over to her, and threw acid in her face. Despite her distress, Maria Alvarez had no trouble recognizing her husband Victor's face under the stocking.

Janet Nicholson eventually made a remarkable recovery, both physically and emotionally. But the wrath of her client's husband cost her the permanent loss of vision in one eye.

7

A TRAGEDY PUBLICIZED

In addition to the shocking Metropolitan Opera House murder, my hypnotic services have been requested on a number of cases that have earned extensive press coverage and widespread public interest. Two of the most fascinating were the Renee Katz subway assault and the rash of cold-blooded shootings at the hands of David Berkowitz, the infamous Son of Sam.

In the face of media scrutiny and citizens' moral outrage, investigators of highly publicized crimes are under tremendous pressure to bag a suspect. For this reason, I was especially pleased to have been able to help pry the lid off these explosive cases.

At about 7:45 A.M. on June 7, 1979, Renee Katz was dozing in her seat in an "E" train on New York's Independent subway line. The rickety cars were speeding along beneath Manhattan's already steaming streets, fast approaching the line's Fiftieth Street

Station. The teen-ager had slept through the Seventh Avenue stop, where she normally changed to the "D" on her way to the High School of Music and Art from her home in Queens. A talented flutist, Renee was nearing the end of her senior year at the highly regarded institution.

As the doors opened at Fiftieth Street, she awoke with a start and bolted out of the train. When she had collected her thoughts, she was annoyed with herself—first, for having fallen asleep and second, for having gotten off. She could have saved time by staying on and continuing to Forty-second Street, where she would have been able to catch an "A" uptown to school. She decided to do just that, rather than go back to Seventh Avenue, and hoped the detour wouldn't make her late for class.

The pretty young woman waited anxiously at the edge of the platform for the next downtown train. When she leaned out over the tracks just three minutes later, she saw an "E" begin its glide into the station. As she focused on the lead car, and was thinking how lucky she was that the train had come so soon, she felt a push on her shoulder. It was really a shove, with enough power behind it to knock her off-balance. To her horror, she found herself sailing off the platform and landing on the tracks, seconds ahead of the careening train.

Renee felt something brush her right arm as she rolled into the crevice beneath the platform overhang. The fortuitous space was her salvation. Her greatest fear was that no one would know she was there. She let out a blood-curdling scream, but ear-piercing as it was, it couldn't compete with the roar of the train rumbling past her at an unnervingly slow rate of deceleration. The leaden behemoth finally came to a stop, its deafening clatter replaced by a woman's high-pitched pleas for help. They were unmistakable to everyone in the station.

Renee had looked at her arm. She dared not believe what she saw: a bleeding stump where the beginning of her hand had been. One of the giant metal wheels had sliced through her wrist.

Renee's screams were echoed by a blaring siren, and in seconds, motorman Justo Barriero was at her side, followed quickly by medics and Transit Authority police. The traumatized young woman's hand was retrieved, and both she and it were rushed to

Bellevue Hospital, where a team of microsurgeons, after hours of laboriously suturing tiny blood vessels and nerves, succeeded in rejoining the hand to Renee's arm.

The Transit Authority investigators hadn't a clue as to who was responsible for knocking the defenseless teen-ager off the platform. The throngs of subway passengers, all eager to know and see what had happened, had provided the perfect refuge, and had foiled any chance of singling out a likely perpetrator. However, the next day, a passenger on the train that had struck Renee came forward. Middle-aged Sally Harper commuted daily to a Manhattan job from her home in Queens. She told the transit police that she had seen a young man racing down the platform, just as her train was pulling into the Fiftieth Street Station.

The witness had caught only a fleeting glimpse of the possible suspect, and the investigators counted on me to wangle a description good enough for a composite. Just five days after the incident, I sat opposite Sally Harper at the transit police's Major Case Squad office in Brooklyn.

After the usual introductory comments, I activated the tape recorder. "Today is June 12, 1979, and the time is 1759 hours. This is Sergeant Charles Diggett of the Chief of Detectives Office and with me are Detective John Morgan and Detective Robert Lonigan of the Transit Authority police, Major Case Squad. We're going to interview Sally Harper of Jamaica, Queens, about an incident that occurred on June 7, 1979, and carried under Major Case number 128.

"Okay, Sally, before I hypnotize you, would you like to tell me in your own words where you were on Thursday, June 7, 1979, at about eight A.M. in the morning?"

"I was on the 'E' going to West Fourth Street. When the train pulled into the Fiftieth Street Station, I happened to turn and look out. I saw a black youth, possibly about sixteen years of age, running down the platform. He was going very fast, and all I could think of was, 'I wonder what he did that he's running so fast?' About thirty seconds later, the train came to a stop, and the motorman told us that there was a female passenger on the tracks. The sirens started screaming and continued until I left the train. A few minutes later, the motorman told us that the passenger was alive. About five or ten minutes later, the police and the medics arrived. As a matter of fact, they passed me. Then the doors to my car opened, and I was able to leave the train."

"Where did you get on this train?"

"At the Van Wyck Station in Queens."

"And how do you get to Van Wyck?"

"I walk about three blocks. The subway is at Queens and Van Wyck Boulevards."

"That's about three blocks from your home?"

"Right."

"Is that your usual routine?"

"Yes, it is."

"So you walk down and get on the same train. Do you have to change trains to get to your destination?"

"I didn't change, but sometimes I do. That day, I continued to West Fourth."

"When you change, where do you do it?"

"At Seventh Avenue. That's one stop before Fiftieth. . . . I got a window seat, and when the train pulled in, I looked out and noticed this boy running very fast."

"Did you notice anyone else running?"

"No, nobody else was running."

"And where did he run to?"

"He was running toward the end of the station. He ran past me."

"Can you tell me what he was wearing?"

"I didn't really notice his clothes. . . . I can't remember what he was wearing."

"Can you tell me if his clothes were light or dark?"

"The colors . . . I really was just looking at his face and thinking he must've done something, or else why would he be running like that?"

"You said you were looking at his face? What can you tell me about it?"

"His hair was curly. . . . He had sort of a full, round face, and I did notice he was slim. . . . I remember his arms swinging up high . . . you know, like helping himself to run faster."

"Did he have anything in his hands?"

"No, nothing in his hands."

"Do you remember what kind of day it was? Warm, cold, raining?"

"It was a muggy, humid day."

"Did this fellow seem to be dressed for that kind of day?"

"Well, I think he was dressed heavily, although I didn't notice any heavy garments . . . but I don't really recall."

"Were people wearing raincoats and carrying umbrellas that day?"

"Yes, Thursday was a bad day."

"Did the fellow have a raincoat on?"

"No, he didn't."

"Did you notice if he had any jewelry on?"

"I didn't see any jewelry, as far as I can remember."

"You said his hair was kind of curly? How long was it?"

"Not long, not cut short either."

"Longer than mine?"

"Your hair isn't curly."

"I'm talking about the length."

"It wasn't long. . . . Don't forget, he ran past me very quickly."

"Did he have enough hair for you to consider it an Afro?"

"It wasn't an Afro."

"How would you describe his nose?"

"Well, I think . . . I'm trying to remember. . . . It was sort of a bulbous-type nose."

"Like W. C. Fields?"

"No, not like that. I just meant the shape was a little roundish."

"Would you describe it as big?"

"He was average, not very tall, not short. He was a kid of average height."

"No, I mean his nose."

"Oh, the nose wasn't . . . It was just a round nose."

"But it was average for his face?"

"Right, it was proportioned. . . . It wasn't jutting out or anything."

"What about his lips?"

"I don't remember them too well. . . . I don't think they were very large, though."

"Did you see his teeth?"

"No."

"Why not? Did he have his mouth closed?"

"I'm not sure if it was closed, but I know his teeth didn't show. If his mouth was open slightly, it wasn't enough to see his teeth."

"He didn't have buck teeth?"

"He definitely did not have. . . ."

"Did you see his ears?"

"I could see an ear for a second. . . . You know, one ear as he was running past me."

"Anything unusual?"

"No."

"What was he wearing?"

"I'm trying to think. I don't want to imagine what I really didn't see. . . . It could've been a little jacket—you know, a short one with a zipper . . . but I'm not sure. . . . I have a feeling it was one of those zip-up, poplin types . . . but I just can't say for sure."

"You have a good memory, Sally, and that's very important to us. If your memory is good to start off with, it'll be that much better under hypnosis. You obviously got a good look at this fellow, didn't you?"

"Yes, mainly his face. That's what I looked at."

"I see. But sometimes we can pick up things we don't realize. . . . For instance, suppose we were having a serious conversation, discussing something we both felt strongly about. If those guys in the other room were to yell something, you probably wouldn't have the slightest idea what it was. Yet under hypnosis, you might be able to remember something about it. . . ."

"I just remembered, he wore sneakers. That's coming back to me. He *did* have sneakers on."

"What color were they?"

"I don't know if I'm just *saying* black or what, but that's what I feel—black. I could be wrong."

It seemed that Sally was avoiding the issue of hypnosis by interrupting with new material as fast as she could. I was going to have to tread softly to ease her out of her anxiety and not frighten her further.

"Okay, Sally, I just want to tell you now that psychologists have found that the mind is like a tape recorder; anything we've ever seen, heard, touched, or smelled is recorded in our subconscious. We don't know for certain that this is valid, but a lot of psychologists feel it is. Suppose we were to meet somewhere a year from now. If I were to say to you, 'Do you remember exactly what questions I asked you a year ago?' you probably wouldn't be able to recall most of them."

"You're telling me."

"But if we played the tape recorder, it would tell us exactly what we said because a tape recorder never forgets. And they say our subconscious never forgets either. The only problem is that we keep piling new information on the old, and a lot of it gets buried down there. Unless something is very important to us, it's often hard to recall it. For instance, if you gave a great deal of thought to last Christmas, you'd probably remember some things about it. Since it comes only once a year, it's pretty memorable to everyone. But if I asked you to think back and tell me what you did on February 17, unless it was your birthday or some other special day, you probably wouldn't remember anything about it. But last Thursday was an important day. I'm sure you won't forget it for as long as you live. Yet some of the details about it are already in your subconscious.

"You and I are talking to each other with our conscious minds, but in the background, the subconscious is picking up interesting bits and pieces. In this relaxed state known as hypnosis, there's a kind of exchange. The subconscious comes forward, and the conscious recedes a bit. Now we're going to find out if this is true for you, with the profile I told you about."

I put Sally through the profile procedures. She ended up with a high score. She had good arm levitation and responded to post-hypnotic suggestion; when I touched her on the elbow, she regained sensation and control in her arm. Asked why her arm had returned to normal, she replied that she didn't know. I could see that she hadn't been consciously aware of my touching her on the predetermined spot, nor did she remember that this was the cue for her arm to function normally again. The response had operated on a subliminal level, proving to me that she was a susceptible subject, and to her that she indeed had been under hypnosis, even though she might feel as if nothing happened. This is why the induction profile is so important a preliminary step. It dissipates skepticism and familiarizes subjects with the true nature of the hypnotic experience, setting them up for even deeper relaxation during the actual interrogation.

After telling Sally how well she had done on the profile, I continued preparing her to permit her recollections to surface easily.

"In this relaxed state, time and space don't mean anything, Sally. You can go forward and back to any date or place you'd like. In a few moments, I'll ask you to let your mind float back there to Thursday, June 7 . . ."

"Must you use the word float? Float to me . . . I'd rather just relax into a slow . . . just loosen up or something."

"All right, Sally, are you relaxed now?"

"Yes."

"Okay, follow along with me. One, look up as far as you can. . . . Two, keep looking up and slowly close your eyes. . . . Take a deep breath. . . . Three, exhale and let your eyes relax, but keep them closed. . . . Let that relaxation spread through your whole body, from the top of your head all the way down, down—over your face, the back of your neck. Let your muscles relax, and let go—your shoulders and your arms, your chest, your stomach, your hips, your knees, your ankles. Just feel yourself letting go more and more."

After continuing with repeated suggestions of relaxation and letting go, I used the standard deepening procedure of counting backward from ten to one. Then, after gently easing Sally back to the preceding Thursday, I cautioned her to speak only in the present tense. I didn't want her just to *remember* seeing that boy. I wanted a genuine re-experiencing of all sensory input during the morning of the tragic incident.

"Under hypnosis, some people are actually able to visualize, moment to moment, occurrences they've experienced. See if you can do it, Sally. See yourself walking to the subway from your house on that warm, muggy day, Thursday, June 7, and tell me this: What are you wearing?"

"I can't remember."

"It's the kind of day that seems like it's about to rain all the time, is that right?"

"Yes."

"Do you have an umbrella?"

"Yes, I do."

"What time is it?"

"It's about seven thirty-five in the morning."

"And when you get to the subway, do you walk downstairs or upstairs?"

"I walk down the steps."

"Do you have a token, or do you have to buy one?"

"I have a token."

"Are you on the platform now?"

"Yes, I'm on the platform."

"What train are you taking?"

"The 'E.'"

"How long do you have to wait?"

"Not long, three minutes."

"Okay, you get on the train. Is it crowded?"

"Not crowded at my station."

"Do you sit down?"

"No. All the seats are taken."

"You're riding along. What's the first stop?"

"Union Turnpike."

"The train stops at Union Turnpike, and people get off. Are you reading?"

"No, just standing and holding on."

"What's the next stop?"

"Seventy-fifth Avenue."

"Do you see anything unusual there?"

"No."

"Okay, the train starts again. What's the next stop?"

"Roosevelt Avenue."

"Are you still standing?"

"Yes."

"And the next stop is . . ."

"Queens Plaza."

"Are you still standing?"

"Yes, and it's getting very crowded."

"And the stop after that?"

"Twenty-third Street and Ely Avenue."

"Do you meet anybody you know?"

"No. There's a girl I see all the time on the train, but I don't know her—just another passenger."

"Does she get off at the same stop you do?"

"No, she goes past my stop."

"What's the next stop?"

"Lexington Avenue."

"And you're still standing?"

"Still standing."

"When do you finally get a seat?"

"Seventh Avenue."

"At last, you get a seat at Seventh Avenue. Where do you sit?"

"Near a window."

"Is the window near your right shoulder or . . ."

"Left shoulder."

"Is the girl you see every morning still on the train?"

"She's standing."

"Near you?"

"Yes."

"Are you coming to the next stop?"

"Yes, Fiftieth Street."

"The train's pulling into Fiftieth Street?"

"Yes, I'm looking out the window. I see this boy running down the platform."

"Stop right there, Sally. Take a good look at him and describe him to me."

"He's black, has curly hair, large eyes, round nose . . . and he's running really fast."

"What's he wearing?"

"I believe a jacket."

"What color?"

"It looks like tan."

"A tan jacket? How long is it?"

"To the waist."

"Does it have any letters or patches on it?"

"No."

"How old do you think he is?"

"He looks about sixteen."

"Does he look at you?"

"I don't think so. He's looking straight ahead . . . as if he wants to get away fast."

"What's happening with the train?"

"The train slows down and stops. We have to wait."

"When the train stops moving, do you see this fellow?"

"No."

"You see him only while the train is moving?"

"Right."

"Where's the girl you see every day?"

"She's standing."

"Does she see him, too?"

"No."

"Why not?"

"I mention to her that I saw a boy running. I thought it odd that he was running like that. And she says, 'You saw a boy?' That's all she says. . . . Then we hear there's a girl . . . a female passenger on the tracks."

"Okay, what I would like you to do now is take a nice, deep breath. . . . That's it, let it out slowly. How well were you able to visualize yourself? Did you see yourself walking? Did you see the boy on the subway platform?"

"I visualized the boy and the subway better than myself going to work."

"Okay, let's see if you can visualize something else. I'd like you to see yourself at home. You're watching television in bed, in a chair, wherever your favorite spot is. See the screen growing brighter. Your favorite program is on. Are you visualizing it now?"

"I don't have a favorite program."

"Okay, pick one out. . . . Are you visualizing it? What is it?"

" 'Barnaby Jones.' "

"Just put your head back and relax. You're nice and comfortable. Really see the 'Barnaby Jones' show. In a moment, I'm going to count back from ten to one. As I count, you keep relaxing more and more. There'll be enough time while I'm counting for you to watch the entire program. When I get to the count of one, the program will end, and a commercial will start."

I counted backward from ten very slowly.

"Now the program is over. Was it a repeat or a new show?"

"It was a repeat."

"Okay, a commercial is coming on. You don't have to pay any attention to it. I want you to listen to me. The next program will be a documentary film showing Sally Harper going to work on June 7, 1979. When I count to three, you'll see yourself at about eight o'clock—as if a television crew had been filming in the subway car. The camera will see everything you see, and you'll tell me about it. One . . . two . . . and three. What's happening?"

"It's quiet. Nothing's happening. Everybody is reading a book, the paper, or just staring. We keep riding and riding. Nothing unusual is happening. Then I get a seat. I'm glad to get a seat, and I'm thinking the train is making good time. I hope there won't be any delays."

"Why? Are you late?"

"No, I'm thinking we're on schedule. No power failures. That's on my mind. I'm happy. Then the train pulls into the Fiftieth Street Station. I'm looking out the window, and I see the boy running."

"When you see him in the best possible way you can, stop the camera. Freeze the action, and take a look at that boy. Can you see him now?"

"Yes."

"Describe him."

"Medium-black skin, curly hair, large eyes, nose full and round. His features are sort of like a baby's, and he's young. Nothing else."

"Close in on his face. What kind of expression does he have?"

"It wasn't a frightened look. There was no expression—maybe just trying to get away from something, that's all."

"If I were an artist, would you be able to describe that face well enough for me to draw it?"

"I think so."

"If you ever see his face again, would you recognize it?"

"I hope so. . . . I'm not sure, but I hope so."

"Okay, Sally, you've done a very good job for us, and we're in good shape. In a few minutes, I'm going to count from one to five, but before I do, let me ask the detectives if they have any questions. Can you get that picture back in your mind?"

"I'm bringing it back. . . . Okay."

The investigators were satisfied. They had no further questions. But I thought I'd try one more time to elicit a better description of the suspect's clothes.

"Let's concentrate on colors. See if you can do it yourself."

"He's wearing a gray jacket . . . sort of a gray-beige."

"Is it open or closed?"

"I don't really know."

"What about the trousers? Are they dark or light?"

"I don't know."

"What about the sneakers?"

"Black."

"Are they low, or do they come up over the ankles like basketball sneakers?"

"They come up over the ankles."

"Do they have an emblem on them of any kind? . . . Back up the film and let it run again. Watch him running. . . . Now watch his feet."

"They're going up really high. He's running fast. . . . I think the soles are white."

"Okay, that's fine. As I said before, I'm going to count to five. When I do, I want you to open your eyes. You'll find that your mind will be clear and alert, and you'll feel relaxed and rested. If we decide to try this again a little later, you'll be even more relaxed because the more you're hypnotized, the better you get at it."

I also suggested to Sally, before returning her to consciousness, that she would remember everything she said during the trance. And I explained the phenomenon of perseveration, urging her to write down any new information that occurred to her.

"Okay, now when I get to five, you'll feel perfect in every way. One, you're emerging now . . . two, you're coming all the way up . . . three, your eyes are beginning to open . . . four, your eyes are open . . . and five, you're wide awake. . . . Feels good, doesn't it? Were you able to relax?"

"Yes, I was. . . . Can I tell you something? My heart was

beating very rapidly when we started. I was really nervous, and trying to relax at the same time. I was so aware of my heartbeat, but later on, I felt myself getting calmer and calmer."

"Most people react that way. They have a fear of the unknown. But when they see how easy it is, they relax."

"Right."

"Were you able to see the TV screen?"

"Yes."

"When you saw this young man, and looked at his face, did it come in clearly?"

"Yes, it did."

"Will you be able to describe it to an artist?"

"Yes, definitely."

"Is there anything more you'd like to go over?"

"No, I'm fine."

"The time is now 1854 hours, and this is the end of the interview."

Hypnosis had helped Sally recapture a strong image of the boy's face, and she supplied the investigators with a good composite. The youthful sprinter was found. I don't know exactly how, but I do know that Sally's sketch was instrumental.

At transit police headquarters, the boy denied being in the Fiftieth Street Station that morning. But when the investigators played the tape of the hypnotic testimony for him, the suspect heard an unmistakable description of himself. He also happened, at that moment, to be wearing the jacket and sneakers recounted by the witness. Realizing he could no longer get away with lying, he admitted being there. He said that, yes, he had seen the assault, and was so frightened by it that he had run out of the station as fast as he could.

In the meantime, an anonymous informant had dropped a dime, and told the police that the man they were looking for was Allen Lewis, a twenty-six-year-old mail clerk. In checking out the tip, the detectives discovered that the name and description given them belonged to a character who had been convicted a number of times of molesting women subway passengers, but never incarcerated. The police put a tail on Lewis to get a handle on his movements to and from work. The Fiftieth Street Station was not one of his customary stops.

There was no way the detectives could put Lewis on that platform on the morning in question—no way, that is, until the boy
who had run away gave them a reasonable description of the
subway masher as the person he had seen shoving the victim.
That was what the investigators were waiting for, and they
arrested Lewis.

The suspect admitted having a penchant for rubbing up
against females in the crowded subways, especially when he had
had an argument with his girl friend. On the basis of the boy
witness' description, a lie detector test, and the suspect's confession—later retracted—that he might have accidentally nudged
Renee onto the tracks, Allen Curtis Lewis was brought to trial in
January of 1980.

A freshman at Queens College at the time, Renee apppeared in
court with her hand heavily bandaged. The victim had endured
five more operations on it, but it had yet to be restored to full
capacity. The young woman had had to learn to write with her
left hand, and I hardly need mention that she could no longer
play the flute. During her emotion-filled testimony on the stand,
Renee was unable to identify Lewis because she had never actually seen her attacker. And, at the moment of truth, the boy who
had been in the station couldn't say that the man pointed out to
him in the courtroom was, without a doubt, the person he had
seen shove the victim off the platform. No other eyewitnesses
had come forward. The shortage of incriminating evidence
resulted in the acquittal of the defendant.

The most interesting aspect of the trial to me was the fact that
the defense attorney had hired a respected hypnotist to put
Lewis into a trance. The counsel then told the court that his client couldn't have been in the station at the time of the assault because this is what his hypnotic deposition had revealed. Either
the lawyer was unaware of the fact that an individual can lie in a
trance state—which is why it is useless, let alone a violation of
rights, to hypnotize a *suspect* as part of an investigation—or the
defense ploy was a deliberate attempt to capitalize on a popular
misconception.

Hypnosis for the defense seems to be a growing trend. As a
means of compensating for the forensic application of the medium, more and more defense attorneys are engaging their own

hypnotists to confirm the innocence of their clients. There's nothing new under the sun, though; the strategy was attempted as early as 1897, but not until recently have judges given it serious consideration. I suppose their recognition of the defense tactic is the unfortunate result of the increased use of hypnosis-derived evidence by the prosecution.

I trust that, as the courts gain a better understanding of the dynamics of hypnosis, they will realize the futility of taking heed of claims made under it by the accused.

As midnight approached, Connie Noresky and Elise Malfitano had had enough. The two seventeen-year-olds had been at Shazam!, a Queens discotheque, since nine, and boredom had begun to set in. They had danced a bit and talked with friends from school, but hadn't met any "cute" guys, and decided it was time to leave.

On the way to Elise's car, parked about a block away, the two ran into a couple of young men they knew from their neighborhood.

"Leaving so soon?" one of the guys asked, with none-too-subtle intent.

"We're going home," Connie demurred, scarcely hiding her indifference.

"It's early. Why don't you two come back and boogie with us?"

"No thanks. Some other time," Connie called out, as she and Elise stepped up their pace toward the car.

Once inside, Connie felt protected. "Boy, those guys are creeps, aren't they?"

"You're telling me," Elise concurred. "I'm glad we got rid of them." She shook her head, started the car, and drove off.

It was one of those hot, muggy nights when the humidity turns the city into a concrete steam bath. Elise's blouse was sticking to her back, and the steering wheel felt clammy as she negotiated the narrow streets lined with parked cars. When she pulled up to the curb in front of Connie's building, she turned the motor off. The two weren't quite ready to part company. The oppressive darkness and stillness of the street was relieved only by their giggling as they shared thoughts about boys and other girlish interests.

After a few minutes, they were aware of a car turning the corner and parking nearby. Connie's parents and a friend of theirs got out, and came over to the two girls. The adults were in a jovial mood.

"Hi, how're you doing?" Connie's father asked.

"Oh, we're fine, just talking," Connie responded, without getting out of the car.

The adults and teen-agers discussed the heat and their respective evenings briefly, before the senior party decided to go into the building.

"Why don't you two come upstairs?" Connie's mother suggested.

"We want to talk some more. I'll be up in a little while," her daughter promised cheerfully. She waved through the car's open window, as the threesome entered the high-rise apartment.

About five minutes later, Connie bid her friend good night. She opened the car door, but something made her freeze. Elise leaned forward, trying to see what was keeping Connie from getting out of the car. Over her friend's shoulder, she barely made out the outline of what appeared to be a man hulking in the darkness. He was crouching, but immediately stood up. A shiver went up Elise's spine, as he took something from his pocket. He raised his arm, and pointed a brown paper bag at Connie.

A shot rang out. Smoke poured from a hole in the bag. Connie was thrown against the back of the seat. Blood streamed down her face. Elise screamed and flailed hysterically, while the assailant pumped bullet after bullet into Connie. One of the last struck Elise in the left thigh. She shrieked louder than ever, and with that, the sinister figure disappeared into the darkness as stealthily as he had materialized.

The young woman's sobs and cries for help echoed through the sullen night air. To the killer's ears, they grew ever fainter, as he retreated further and further from the scene.

Connie Noresky was among the Son of Sam's first homicide victims. A total of six would eventually be attributed to the notorious gunman whose murderous rampage spread from Queens to the Bronx and Brooklyn. The elusive assassin had all of New York City terrorized and the police baffled for one whole year during 1976 and 1977. He came to be called the .44-Caliber Killer because of the bullets retrieved from the murdered or wounded victims. Ballistics determined that the projectiles were fired from the same short-barreled, .44 revolver. It was the kind of weapon that could be concealed easily, yet was capable of delivering a powerful wallop.

In all but one or two of the eight known attacks, the fugitive's MO was naggingly consistent. He stalked couples in areas that customarily attracted love-making in parked cars. Approaching unnoticed from the rear, he fired through the front passenger window at the women usually seated there, sometimes wounding, and in one case, killing, the men in the driver's seat. The deranged criminal prowled at night, most of the attacks occurring after midnight, and his female targets were all young, ranging in age from seventeen to twenty-six.

In a thumb-nose gesture that further infuriated the already frustrated investigators, the killer sent a note to the department. In it, he chided the lawmen for failing to capture him, and insisted that his actions were the bidding of one "Sam, a six-thousand-year-old reincarnated demon," who ordered the killings through his howling black dog. Hence, the handle, Son of Sam, that was picked up greedily by the media. The investigators had the foresight not to reveal to the press how the letter was signed. When they finally snared the suspect, this would become the one fail-safe means of determining that the man in custody was the true multiple murderer. Only the real writer of the message could know what he had so appropriately called himself.

The menace to the city sent another note to columnist Jimmy Breslin, this time boasting that he held the murder weapon with two hands, firing it in regulation police style—crouched with legs apart. The information further hampered the investigation by casting suspicion among the ranks. In a distasteful display of comradely betrayal, policemen tailed off-duty cohorts and retired members of the force, and reported their whereabouts.

These were dim moments, but as disparate forces united in a single purpose, the investigation became one of the department's shining hours. More than seven hundred officers volunteered off-duty time to help, and one hundred and thirty-six men laid off during budget cutbacks were ordered rehired by the mayor. In all, two hundred and twenty-five men in uniform and seventy-five detectives worked full time, tracking down leads and prowling neighborhoods that were likely to come under siege. They even resorted to propping decoy dummies in parked cars, baiting a series of traps for the unsuspecting animal. But he wasn't to be fooled that easily.

Eying the thirty-one-thousand-dollar reward, lunatics of every description crawled from the woodwork to turn informant. At one point, the task-force headquarters set up at Shea Stadium processed as many as a hundred calls an hour. The unstinting investigators checked out more than five thousand named as perpetrators, and ended up putting fifteen hundred of the most likely suspects under surveillance.

The manhunt hadn't yet reached these massive proportions when I was called over to the 109th Precinct in Queens at the end of August 1976, to hypnotize Elise Malfitano. The investigators were having difficulty with the young witness, and thought I might be able to coax a description from her. She was expectedly disconsolate and shaken in the wake of her best friend's cruel demise and the violence she herself had narrowly survived. Like most of the near-victims who were witness to the suspect's viciousness, Elise was afraid of the consequences if she co-operated with the police. And she still hadn't been able to turn her thoughts to that awful moment, let alone contemplate the killer's face, and describe it.

Sobbing and trembling were the only responses to the detectives' questions, and the witness adamantly refused to be hypnotized when it was suggested. Finally, about a month after the assault, she was persuaded to help bring the culprit to justice, and after she had been assured that reliving the incident would be less painful under hypnosis, she agreed to the interview.

I was introduced to a pretty young woman, who showed no sign of the physical injury she had sustained. But her face was tear-stained, and she was obviously frightened. Her greeting to me was unintelligible. In my gentlest manner, I worked very hard to ease her fears and help her relax as much as she could, considering the circumstances. She was so distracted that it took a consummate effort just to get her into a very light trance. When I was certain I couldn't prod her to go any deeper, I used the imagery of pages flying off the calendar in reverse to prepare her to confront that tragic night.

". . . That's it, Elise, go back in time to July 31 . . . thirtieth . . . now it's July 29, 1976, a very important day. What were you doing that afternoon?"

"I got home from summer classes, had something to eat, and called my friend to tell her I was going to the disco that night. Connie came over later, and agreed to go to Shazam! with me. . . . We went to my car. . . . Connie said she had to tell her brother where she was going. We found him on Hill Street. Connie told him to tell her parents where she'd be and that she'd be home about midnight. He said to be careful. . . . We took Brookview Road to the parkway. . . . Parked around the corner from Shazam! . . . We went into the disco. Joe was at the door collecting the money. . . . We walked around, talking to friends."

"Good, Elise, you're doing very well. Now listen to me. Take a deep breath, and let it out slowly . . . slowly . . . That's it. Any time you become the least bit upset, take a deep breath, and let it out gradually, like that. It'll help calm you. Remember, we'll stop any time you want to. . . ."

"I was talking to Allan Landau, a good friend of mine from school."

"Okay, what happens then?"

"Nothing's working out, so we leave. . . . We see two creepy guys from our neighborhood. . . . They try to pick us up. We say no. . . . We go back to the car, and take off."

"Do you go directly to Connie's house?"

"Yes."

"Look around, Elise. Do you see anyone on the street?"

I waited for a response. The witness had begun sobbing softly, but it didn't seem to be disturbing her trance.

"Take your time. If you think you feel strong enough, continue with the story."

"Cars are going by . . . kids usually hanging out on the corner, but no one there tonight. . . . It was too hot that night."

"This is about twelve-twenty?"

"Yes. . . . I'm talking with Connie. . . . A van passes by down the block. . . . Connie's mother and father pull up in a car. A guy named Bob is with them. Her parents come over to the car. They're smiling and laughing. . . . They talk to us for a while. They want us to come up. . . . They leave. We watch them walk into the elevator. . . . Connie is about to get out of the car. She opens the door. Stops . . . I look past her and see this person on the sidewalk."

"Can you see him clearly?"

"Yes."

"Is the street well lighted?"

"There's light on the other side."

"Can you see his features? . . . If you see him again, will you know him?"

"Yes."

"Have you ever seen him before?"

"No."

"Anyone in Shazam! look like him?"

"No. I know them all by sight, by their faces."

"The first time you see this man, what's he doing?"

"Looking at the car."

"Where are his hands?"

"Uh . . . at his sides."

"How do you feel? . . . When you first see him, are you afraid?"

"A little bit. I was going to pull away with the car because he looked suspicious."

"Something odd about him?"

"The way he appeared . . . from nowhere."

"What does he look like?"

"Staring. . . . He was staring at us."

"What about his clothes? Was he dressed like others in the neighborhood?"

"Yeah. . . . He was dressed casually."

"What does he do now?"

"He takes something out of his pocket . . . stands up . . . raises his arm quickly . . . holding something in his hand."

"Which hand?"

"Right hand."

"What is it?"

"A bag."

"What color?"

"Brown paper."

"Can you tell which hand he's shooting with?"

Elise's voice caught in her throat. She was too upset to answer. I changed the question.

"The first time you see the gun, is it pointed at you?"

"He was firing. He raised his hands and fired!"

Elise shouted this last, before collapsing in tears. I tried to console her, empathizing with her ordeal and praising her bravery and the fine job she had done for us. Despite her agitation, her eyes had remained closed and she appeared to be in a very light trance. After I had succeeded in calming her somewhat, we talked about other things—school, her plans for the future—for a bit. Then I asked if she would permit me to try another procedure, again promising we would stop if she felt the slightest discomfort. Elise expressed her willingness to go on. I wondered if the beach imagery would help her fall into a more relaxed state.

"Do you like the beach, Elise?"

"Yes, very much. . . . I wish I was there right now."

"You are. You're walking along the most beautiful beach you've ever seen. The sky is a brilliant blue, the soaring palm trees are swaying in the gentle breeze, and the warming sun on your skin makes you feel good all over. Can you feel the sun and the ocean breezes?"

"Yes."

"Do they make you feel better?"

"Yes, they do."

"Good. You deserve this relaxing day at the seashore. Leave all your cares behind. Just let yourself go, and drink in the sun's rays, the smell of the ocean, and the sound of the surf. . . . Do you see that big puddle up ahead, left by the outgoing tide?"

"Yes, I see it."

"I want you to walk up to it and dip your big toe into the water. Can you feel how hot it is from the sun shining on it?"

"Yes."

"Stir the water up a bit with your toe, and then take it

out. . . . Watch the ripples as they begin to smooth. . . . When the water is completely still, you'll see an image forming in it. . . . Can you see anything?"

"Yes . . . something. . . ."

"It's becoming clearer and clearer. . . . Now it's so sharp that you can make out what it is. . . . It's the face of the man who shot you."

Elise immediately put her hand up in front of her own face, as if to protect herself, and exclaimed, "No, no, I don't want to see it!" She started to cry, but I took her hand in mine, and compelled her to listen to me.

"It's all right, Elise, it's all right. You don't have to see it. Just calm down and listen to the sound of my voice. . . . Take a deep breath. . . . Let it out slowly. . . . That's the way, relax. . . . There's nothing to fear. . . . You're beginning to feel a lot better . . . calmer . . . more secure. . . ."

I brought Elise out of her trance, after suggesting that she would be alert, refreshed, and much less afraid than she had been at the beginning of the interview. When she opened her eyes, she smiled for the first time, and seemed very relieved.

I concluded that I hadn't succeeded in persuading the witness to take a long, hard look at her assailant. But when her session with the sketch artist was over, the investigators had a good likeness of a round-faced, cherubic-looking, curly-haired man. Hypnosis had apparently helped Elise evoke a clearer picture than I had imagined.

A witness to a subsequent .44-caliber homicide supplied the investigators with a sketch that was totally at odds with Elise's. It depicted a thin-faced man with straight hair, some of it covering one eye. In light of the new description, the detectives toyed with the idea that there might be two killers. But they abandoned the theory quickly, and decided to go with the composite of the thin-faced man. It ran in the papers, and copies of it were circulated everywhere, including one hundred and sixty thousand to weapon and ammunition outlets across the country. But nothing came of the effort, and the killings continued.

The Son of Sam's final victim was twenty-year-old Stacy Moskowitz. Robert Violante, also twenty and with her at the time, lost the sight of one eye as a result of the well-publicized,

August 1977 ambush at Gravesend Bay in Brooklyn. On that early morning, around 2:30 A.M., forty-nine-year-old Cacilia Davis was walking her dog in the area. She happened to catch sight of a man getting out of a 1970 Ford Galaxie sedan, before he disappeared down the street. Minutes later, she saw a policeman ticketing the car. It had been defiantly parked at a fire hydrant. When Ms. Davis read about the homicide, she remembered the suspicious-looking man and the ticketed car, parked just one block from the site of the murder. She contacted the police, and a copy of the summons was secured. The license number recorded on it was traced to a vehicle properly registered in the name of one David Berkowitz, a Yonkers resident.

The .44-Caliber Killer's fatal mistake was that he hadn't resorted to rigging the getaway car with stolen plates. The tan Ford was sitting in front of his apartment building on August 10, 1977, when a police stakeout arrived. The men examined the car and found a semi-automatic rifle on the back seat. Berkowitz eventually emerged from the building. When he got into his car, he was seized, and a year-long homicide spree was over.

The twenty-four-year-old postal worker's only response was spoken calmly, with a sly grin on his face: "Well, I guess you got me. What took you so long?" When asked how he had signed his childishly scrawled communiqué, he answered with fiendish accuracy, "The monster."

The one-time army sharpshooter held onto his story that demons had commanded him to kill. Two examining psychiatrists judged the demented killer to be psychotic and mentally unfit to stand trial. But the court accepted a third psychiatrist's opinion: Though behaviorally disordered, Berkowitz was legally sane.

In May of 1978, the two-hundred-and-fifty-six-dollar-a-week mail sorter pleaded guilty to the murder of Stacy Moskowitz and five further counts of murder in the second degree, despite his two attorneys' insistence that he plead not guilty by reason of insanity. Bronx Supreme Court Justice William Kapelman sentenced Berkowitz to twenty-seven prison terms, totaling five hundred and forty-seven years. The many lifetimes of incarceration notwithstanding, the criminal would be eligible for parole after serving just twenty-five years. However, the judge included in his decision a recommendation that Berkowitz never be paroled. Unfortunately, to a review board a quarter century hence, the stipulation will not be legally binding.

The killer is now serving his multiple terms at Attica prison, separated from other inmates. In February of 1979, he called a press conference there to announce that he had totally fabricated his story of demons, howling dogs, and Sam, based on real-life neighbor Sam Carr and his black Labrador retriever.

Looking at the chubby, ironically cherubic face in the picture that ran with the item in the papers, I was reminded again how much Berkowitz's features approximated those in the composite provided by Elise Malfitano; the man bore absolutely no resemblance to the drawing that was widely circulated.

8

A TORCH PASSED

As a follow-up to every hypnotic interrogation, the detective in charge of the investigation is sent an evaluation sheet. When one comes back with a comment such as, "Without hypnosis, I never could have gotten to the bottom of this case"—and many of them do—the sense of accomplishment I feel is immeasurable, not only because my specialty has succeeded again in helping track down a criminal, but because I know that one more individual has been brought into the fold. One more law-enforcement professional has been converted from skeptic to loyal defender of the power of hypnosis.

Spreading the word has become almost as much a part of my job as assisting investigators. Little by little in the last few years, forensic hypnosis has come of age, and at the risk of being accused of blowing my own horn, no small part of that development is the result of my dogged persistence.

The long-held dream of an in-house hypnosis education program is today a reality. I am a permanent fixture on the Police Academy curriculum. Not a single recruit is sworn into the department without having been to one of my lecture/demonstrations. These are in no way meant to train people to be hypnotists, but simply to familiarize them with the state of the art, to dispel the myths and outline the options available to them as future investigators. It is satisfying to know that, to growing legions of new policemen, hypnosis is no longer an unknown to be feared and ridiculed. I look forward to the time when the department is entirely populated by hypnotically sophisticated personnel.

Seasoned investigators can take in any of the lectures I frequently give to various law-enforcement organizations within the city and in surrounding communities. One example is the ninety-minute briefing I regularly conduct as part of the department's week-long homicide course.

Admittedly, I get a big kick out of holding forth at these gatherings and stating the case for the forensic application of hypnosis. At nearly every lecture the scenario is the same: When I arrive, the meeting room is vibrating with expectancy. Grumbling from the more cynical of the group reaches my ear: "Is he gonna tell us this hypnosis bullshit can solve cases? This I gotta see." But by the time demonstrations of arm levitation and other hypnotic marvels are over and the possibilities pondered, the show-me attitude has given way to feverish excitement. Before I can leave, a phalanx of detectives, jackets off, guns strapped under their arms, rushes up and surrounds me. A stranger on the scene might conclude I am about to be seized and carried away. But the men are only eager to know more, to ask about problem cases, to thank me for setting them straight. In the week or so following any given lecture, it isn't unusual for two or three of the men and women who were there to phone and ask me to hypnotize a witness or victim for them.

The arm levitation business is usually the highlight of every session. It is actually a demonstration of one of the tests that make up the Hypnotic Induction Profile, the measure of a subject's degree of suggestibility. The induction procedure I select to hypnotize a subject depends on how easily he can be hypnotized, as indicated by his score on the HIP.

I start the demonstration by having all of the people in the group stand up and extend their arms in front of them at shoulder level. I tell them, "Turn your left hand palm up and point the thumb of your right hand at the ceiling. Now close your eyes and imagine you're supporting the Manhattan telephone directory in your left hand and your right thumb is tied with a string to a giant balloon filled with helium. You can feel your left hand getting heavier and heavier and your right, lighter and lighter."

Slowly but surely the arms of the people in the room start to move apart—one up and the other down. In most cases, those who end up with their arms farthest apart are the best hypnotic subjects. I find that the response distribution is usually about the same for any large group—20 per cent with a good reaction, 60 per cent in the medium range, and 20 per cent reacting poorly—and suspect that the general population would reflect a similar breakdown.

Clued in by the notoriety about my work in the national media and along the investigative grapevine, law-enforcement agencies all over the country have contacted the Chief of Detectives seeking my services. The chief has yet to say no to a single request. More accurately, I should say Inspector Rose has never turned anyone down. He is the one actually responsible for this kind of administrative detail—personnel management, statistics—and he has been more than generous in loaning me out. As long as I am not needed in New York and the outside agency is willing to pick up all travel, hotel, and meal tabs, I am given the go-ahead without question. The same holds true for independent law-enforcement groups within the metropolitan area, such as the Transit Authority police. Although permission to work with these organizations is a mere formality, technically I don't have the authority to say yes, and refer even these requests to Inspector Rose.

Working with agencies in other parts of the country has been a broadening and stimulating opportunity, and I regret the fact that these outings inevitably will be less and less frequent in the future. Invitations to lecture, no doubt, will continue to come in, but as more and more departments enlist their own trained hypnotists, the need for my services will lessen.

Dr. Martin Reiser schedules his course in forensic hypnosis on the West Coast once every three months. Each of these is attended by anywhere from thirty to fifty people from various law-enforcement agencies. So a conservative yearly estimate of the number of police departments adding hypnotists trained by Dr. Reiser to their rosters is a hundred and twenty. The Ethical Hypnosis Training Center in South Orange, New Jersey, likewise, graduates about that many officers every year. This gives us an annual ballpark figure of two hundred and forty men and women. And this amount represents only the two major training sources; I haven't taken into account other accredited institutions offering courses in hypnosis. Understandably, not all of the people who are sent away to be trained come back to their home bases avowed practitioners ready to mesmerize the nearest witness. A small percentage takes advantage of the out-of-town tour just for the pleasure of the trip, all expenses paid. While it is impossible to calculate exactly how many American agencies set up new forensic hypnosis units each year, it wouldn't be out of line to say that the figure is at least three hundred and fifty.

Interest in the new forensic tool hasn't been confined to this country. Scores of foreign agencies, including the Northwest Mounted Police and Scotland Yard, have contacted me from all over the world. They are curious about the effectiveness of the New York program and how it was set up. An inspector from Scotland Yard actually came here and spent a week with me to get a firsthand look at our operation. He went back to England with plenty of food for thought, but before he left, I made sure he got both sides of the picture. I sent him to Dr. Orne, who I knew would fill him in on the evils of policemen practicing hypnosis. I have since lost contact with my British colleague, but doubtless he put his money on the capabilities of professional investigators like himself. He was an intelligent man.

In going about the business of building a broad base of open-mindedness among the department's rank and file, I have kept a vigilant eye out for a potential successor. I have racked up enough years of service to the city to make retirement an imminent possibility. It is incredible how quickly the years have slipped by. I have always looked forward to a house on the water, complete with dock and boat, somewhere south of here, and it is hard to believe that the dream is now just around the corner. Although retirement from active duty will mean more time for the recreational pastimes I enjoy, I can't imagine a life, even then, without hypnosis. In the last few years I have maintained a practice in the therapeutic aspect of the discipline at my home in Babylon on Long Island. Wherever I settle in the future, I intend to continue this work, along with meeting lecture and consultation demands. But I couldn't walk away from the New York program a happy man until I had ironed out a few wrinkles.

One of these was the problem of hypnotizing non-English-speaking subjects. An unexpected dividend came out of the process of devising a solution—a person who I am confident will be able to take my place when I retire.

I first met Millagro Markman at the outdoor range at Rodman's Neck. While I was up there one day, an attractive, young female patrolman approached me, introduced herself, and expressed an interest in hypnosis. She asked if it could help her quit smoking, and I assured her that the chances were excellent that it could. But more important, she asked a number of questions about my work in the program and wondered what her chances were of becoming involved in it. I recommended she get some training, Harry Arons' course in particular, and that was the end of our conversation.

I didn't think about Millie again until roughly six months later, while in the throes of trying to figure out how to communicate with Spanish-speaking subjects. The only way to go that I could think of was to use an interpreter. My remarks to the subject during the induction and actual interview would be in English, the interpreter would translate my words into Spanish and, in turn, would translate the subject's responses. The setup seemed unwieldy at best, and I had grave doubts that it would work. Could I succeed in hypnotizing an individual who wouldn't be in direct contact with me, and would be understanding only the words of a go-between?

There was only one way to find out. I had to get hold of an

interpreter, preferably a bilingual police officer to save the department an outside professional's fee. I immediately thought of Officer Markman. Although she spoke English without a trace of an accent, Millie had told me she was born in Puerto Rico and had settled here as a child. She was a ten-year veteran of the force and was married to Captain Mike Markman of the 41st Precinct, the Bronx's notorious Fort Apache. At the time we met, her tour of duty was also in the Bronx in the Community Affairs Division. She had originally joined the force because she had felt a need to work within the system in behalf of Hispanics. In Community Affairs, she was acting as liaison between the department and the Spanish-speaking community, responding to complaints about the police, resolving disputes, and generally attempting to cement relations between the two groups. I figured she must still be able to understand and speak Spanish. On the phone she assured me she was quite fluent in the language. She also told me that, since she had last spoken to me at the range, she had taken my advice and studied with Harry Arons. She had learned a great deal and had discovered, to her delight, that she was a highly suggestible subject. Through hypnosis she had managed to quit smoking; nothing else had ever worked. Encouraged by these indications of the seriousness of her interest, I arranged with Chief Sullivan to have Millie come to my office to participate in an experiment.

Because of Millie's susceptibility to hypnosis, I decided to change my original plan. Instead of enlisting her ability to interpret, I asked her to take on the role of subject. She was more than willing to assist in any way she could. Anxious for the experiment to succeed, I wanted to have as much going for me as possible. With an easily hypnotized subject, I would at least have the variable of suggestibility licked. Whether or not the subject went under had to depend solely on the success or failure of the intermediary setup. A Spanish-speaking clerk at headquarters agreed to act as interpreter. Although she admitted her Spanish was a little rusty, we went ahead with the experiment just the same.

We were an unlikely threesome. In a close huddle with the two women in my office, I began the hypnotic induction. The pace was painfully slow. Millie eventually did go under but with much greater difficulty than if I had been working with her alone. When the exercise was over, she explained that she had been distracted by the interpreter's fractured Spanish, and was correcting it repeatedly in her mind. I was pleasantly surprised that, despite the cumbersomeness of the whole thing, it had produced results. It was only while mulling over the exercise hours later that it occurred to me that my optimistic assessment was erroneous and the test had proven nothing. Since Millie understood English as well as she did Spanish, she couldn't help overhearing my hypnotic suggestions and mentally responding to them before they were translated. This may or may not have been the case, but because the possibility existed, no concrete conclusion could be drawn. So much for that particular experiment.

A few weeks later, I had an opportunity to try again. I was called down to hypnotize a rape victim. The frightened young woman was Hispanic, and couldn't speak or understand a word of English. Once more, I made a request through channels for Millie's assistance. This time I had the good sense to put her talent as an interpreter to work. For all our efforts, though, we weren't able to coax the victim into even a light hypnotic trance. I learned later that the intermediary setup is occasionally successful, but at the time, the scheme showed all the signs of being a lost cause. This was certainly no fault of Millie's. In fact, I took careful note of what seemed to me to be an impressive performance. Not only was she a responsive and facile interpreter, but she spoke evenly and compellingly, was sensitive to the subject's shifts of mood, and generally exhibited many of the qualities of a potentially excellent hypnotist.

Millie continued her work at Community Affairs, but we kept in close contact. Still holding fast to the dream of eventually working full time for the Hypnosis Unit, she took two courses at the Ethical Hypnosis Training Center, and studied with Dr. Spiegel at the Columbia College of Physicians and Surgeons. She was fast following in my footsteps; I, too, had been trained at both institutions, among others.

Millie had the necessary talent to be a hypnotist and now much of the training. All that remained was experience. I came up with another one of my schemes. I decided to try to have her transferred to the unit as my assistant. True, I had an ulterior motive, but it wasn't as if I didn't really need help. I was bogged down in paperwork, and longed for a typist who could relieve me of my form filling, filing, and scheduling duties. Millie was nimble-fingered at the typewriter, but more significant, having her around would give her the opportunity of developing her hypnotic skill by watching and doing.

But my superiors were well aware of what I was up to, and a herd of wild horses couldn't move them to appoint an assistant hypnotist, at least not until Millie had proven herself an indispensable part of the program. With two major homicide cases, she got her chance.

John and Elizabeth Chen had pork chops for breakfast—not the customary early-morning fare for most Americans, but Mr. and Mrs. Chen were recent immigrants from Taiwan. They were both in their early twenties and thankful to be employed at their relatives' Chinese food take-out establishment in Brooklyn. Elizabeth was four months' pregnant with the couple's first child, and the steady income she and her husband enjoyed made her secure in the knowledge that her baby would be well provided for.

The morning of October 4, 1979, followed a familiar pattern. Shortly after the pair had cleared the kitchen table at the back of the shop and washed their breakfast dishes, Elizabeth began the laborious chopping that is the inevitable starting point of most Chinese dishes. John swept the floors, tidied the customer area, organized the food containers, and then joined his wife.

At around 11:30 A.M., everything was in order. John unlocked the front door and went back to the kitchen ready for the day's first customers. Elizabeth slid behind the counter.

No sooner had she opened the cash register to deposit the day's start-up funds than the front door swung open. Two men, unmasked and both carrying shotguns, swept into the store.

"Okay, hand it over, honey," one of them demanded.

Maybe because he needed something from the front area, but more likely because he had overheard the harsh words and sensed the danger in them, John came out of the kitchen and stood at his wife's side.

"Don't worry, dear, they're not real guns," he reassured her in rapid Chinese.

The two laughed nervously to each other, but the high-pitched sound of giggling was rudely interrupted by an ear-shattering explosion. Blood splattered everywhere and John was thrown back violently against the wall behind the counter, before his body slumped lifelessly to the floor.

Elizabeth's drawn-out, agonized scream was loud enough to be heard for blocks. Her husband's face had literally been blown away. As the cruel reality of the grisly image and the devastating loss it represented sank in, she nearly fainted. Instead, she was overcome by nausea and vomited. The distressed young woman had been oblivious to the fact that the perpetrators had run out the door the instant the fatal blast had found its mark. They hadn't stolen a cent.

The next day, I got a call from one of the two detectives covering the case. He explained that he had been trying to get a couple of descriptions from a woman who had witnessed her husband's homicide. She was extremely upset, new to this country from Taiwan, and spoke very little English. What's more, she was pregnant. He had had no luck with her at all and was going to have to close the case if she couldn't describe the perpetrators. Did I think hypnosis might help calm her down?

"Sure," I said, "bring her over and I'll see what I can do." But after I had hung up, it occurred to me that the witness might find it more comfortable to talk to another woman rather than a man. I rang up Millie and said, "How's your Chinese, kid?"

"What do you mean, Chinese? You know I only speak Spanish," she replied with a laugh.

We had become practiced by now in the kind of mutual ribbing that policemen, like doctors and nurses, indulge in to relieve some of the tension that goes with the profession. In a more serious vein, I outlined the situation and asked if she could come down the next day and give us a hand. I assured her that I would take care of clearing it with the high command.

"I'd be glad to," she replied. "Nothing short of an earthquake could keep me away."

At eleven o'clock the next morning, Elizabeth Chen appeared at my office in the company of her sister and two investigators. Mrs. Chen moved as if in a daze and her eyes were red and puffy.

I told the detectives about Officer Markman and my gut feeling that we would be more likely to get the witness to relax and supply us with the information we wanted if Millie conducted the interview. They had no objections. I was getting a little concerned, though, that it was already eleven-fifteen and there was still no sign of Millie. I called Community Affairs, and was told she was on her way.

By eleven-thirty, I decided we had waited long enough. It was time to swing into action and see if I could accomplish anything on my own. I walked over to Mrs. Chen and said, "How do you do, my name is Sergeant Diggett."

She immediately burst into tears.

With her sister's help, I tried to comfort her, but she shrank away from me in fear. There was no use continuing. No matter how long it took, we would just have to wait until Millie arrived.

I breathed a sigh of relief as Millie walked through the door a few minutes later. I introduced her to the two detectives and, as discreetly as possible, indicated which of the two women was the witness. She walked over to Mrs. Chen and, noticing her condition, thought she would allay some of her fear with a kind remark: "How nice that you're going to have a baby. Would you like it to be a boy or a girl?"

At this, Mrs. Chen again starting crying hysterically.

Realizing I had neglected to tell Millie that the homicide victim was the witness' husband, I drew her aside and explained more of the circumstances surrounding the crime. She went back to the two women, and the detectives and I retreated to the opposite end of the room.

With painstaking patience and warm compassion, Millie succeeded in getting Mrs. Chen to calm down. Repeating herself over and over until she was sure the distraught woman understood what she was saying, she asked her if she could remember what the assailant and his accomplice looked like. In a barely audible voice, Mrs. Chen said yes, she wanted to tell us about them.

A complete change came over the witness. She was growing more relaxed and animated. Millie was working wonders. She explained a little about hypnosis in the simplest terms possible. Despite the language barrier, Mrs. Chen eventually showed signs of comprehending something of the procedure she would be undergoing.

Millie began the induction by telling the witness to relax, take it easy, breathe deeply—anything appropriate she could think of within the confines of the most rudimentary English. This went on for almost a half-hour. I could see Millie's frustration building, but in a thoroughly professional manner, she held on to her concentration and didn't miss a beat.

Miraculously, the subject went into a very light trance. Grateful for small miracles, Millie wasn't about to push her luck and go for a deeper state. She asked the witness to see a picture of the intruders in her mind and describe them for us. Mrs. Chen began to talk about the men's physical characteristics, but her voice was so soft that Millie had to ask her to repeat everything she said. Though the recorder microphone was no more than an inch from her mouth and the volume level was as high as it could go, we discovered later that the tape hadn't picked up a single comprehensible word of her testimony.

Nevertheless, descriptions of the two men gradually emerged. The detectives listened intently and took careful notes. When the interview was over, they were as happy as larks. Mrs. Chen hadn't supplied them with as clear a picture of the two men as they would have liked, but the important thing was that she was now willing to talk about the incident and could assure the investigators that she was able to see a vivid mental image of the perpetrators.

What the detectives hadn't told me at the time was that they had another witness up their sleeve. On the morning of the homicide, someone on the street had caught a glimpse of the two men fleeing from the Chens' shop. Mrs. Chen's descriptions, sketchy as they were, matched this other witness'. Even before the hypnotic interview, the cagey investigators had had a strong suspicion of the identities of the perpetrators. The suspects both had previous arrest records.

The day after Mrs. Chen had undergone hypnosis, the detectives had her take a look at a photo lineup. They slipped the suspects' pictures among two dozen others. The witness was able to pick out the two men the first time through. The suspects were found, taken into custody, and an in-the-flesh lineup was set up. Without hesitation, Mrs. Chen fingered the same two men.

Days before the suspects were scheduled to come to trial, the star witness gave birth to a deformed child. Whether or not the condition of the baby had anything to do with the trauma the woman had experienced as an expectant mother no one can say. The fact remains that the shock of the infant's imperfection was too much for the already devastated widow, and she suffered a complete emotional collapse. No sooner had she recovered a few months later than the baby died. This brought on a relapse even worse than the original breakdown. Unable to endure any more, the young woman became suicidal, and, at this writing, is in a hospital under constant surveillance.

Without Mrs. Chen's testimony, the case against the two men is hopeless. The trial has been postponed until such time as the witness is well enough to testify. The suspected killers have been released on fifty thousand dollars bail each, and if the young widow never recovers, they will be free men.

On her first time out, Millie had done a crackerjack job. I was very proud of her and more certain than ever that the program was in desperate need of the unique capabilities of a woman like herself.

In interviewing women who had suffered the indignity of sexual assault, I often felt the victims might have spoken more openly if I were not a man. By the time they were brought to me, they had already been through the embarrassment of describing the incident at least once to an investigator. When I asked if they minded going through it again, in most cases, they said no. But I couldn't help feeling they weren't all that happy about it and would have been less likely to hold something back, significant or not, if allowed the confidence of a female. I was sure that, with all my sensitivity, only a woman could truly empathize with the victims' ordeal. Watching Millie gain the trust of the sex-crime victims she hypnotizes has confirmed my intuition.

Two months after the Chen killing, a second case requiring Millie's assistance came on the docket. It was a multiple homicide and one of the most brutal crimes I have encountered in all my years of service to the department.

It was cold and snowy on the evening of December 11, 1979. Responding to a report of homicide, Detectives Gregory Matlin and Joseph Bello pulled up in front of a brownstone in East Harlem. With guns drawn, they bounded up the steps of the six-floor walk-up. On the top floor, some of the occupants of the building were milling about in the hallway. Spotting the two lawmen, they motioned excitedly toward the door to one of the apartments. It was half open.

The intrepid pair readied themselves for a possible confrontation with a killer. One of the men crept cautiously into the apartment while the other kept him covered from just outside the doorway.

At first Detective Matlin thought he was hallucinating. He blinked a few times, but the scene of bloody mayhem before him refused to go away. It was enough to send shivers up the spine of the most hardened homicide investigator. As if a team of scalpel-wielding surgeons had suddenly gone berserk, the walls, floors, and furniture were covered with blood, and there were bodies everywhere, contorted into every conceivable attitude. But they all had one thing in common: their throats had been slit from ear to ear.

Having ascertained that there wasn't anyone alive in the apartment, the two men were confident that there was no immediate threat to their own survival. They put their guns away and surveyed the gruesome bloodbath once more. Though they guessed the number of dead to be at least a dozen, the final count came to a grand total of seven—six men and one woman.

The investigation that followed turned up the information that the apartment had been rented in the names of Victor and Elena Guzman, the identities of two of the corpses found at the scene. Originally from Panama, the couple were members of one of the more prominent "families" among New York's illicit drug dealers. Apparently, the mass slaying was the culmination of one family's vendetta against another, a not uncommon pastime in the ruthlessly competitive and unsavory narcotics underworld.

Among the five unfortunates who had accompanied the Guzmans in the way of all flesh were pushers and users who happened to be making purchases at the wrong time.

The investigators had a witness. She was a young woman named Dolores Rodriguez, and she had been around the block, as we say of street characters well versed in the ways of crime. Dolores lived with the Guzmans, and she was promised immunity from prosecution as a dealer if she could supply the investigators with some information about the rubout. Dolores was only too willing to talk.

Also a Panamanian by birth, the woman was herself a heroin addict. She never had to worry about where the next fix was coming from because she was the Guzmans' taster. Whenever a new supply came in, Dolores was shot up, and the stuff's purity was evaluated by the intensity of her high.

She told the team of investigators that she hadn't been at the scene at the time of the murders. Stoned on junk, she had left the apartment with the Guzmans, she to buy cigarettes and Elena and Victor to do some wash at a nearby laundromat. Halfway to the store at the end of the block, she saw two cars she thought she recognized, but couldn't remember from where. They sped past her in the direction of the apartment, and she turned to see where they were going. They stopped next to Elena and Victor. Four men jumped out of the cars, grabbed the couple, and took them forcibly to the brownstone, up its steps and through the door.

Dolores was petrified. Fearful that the thugs would come after her, too, she ran to the subway entrance at the corner and stumbled down the steps into the station. She stayed there until she passed out. When she came to the next morning, she went back to the apartment, where she met up with the police.

The detectives wanted descriptions of the murdered couple's abductors. Dolores tried to remember what they looked like, but she said she was so high at the time that her vision was blurred. She supplied the investigators with some general information about the men's appearances. It was hardly enough for any concrete leads.

The investigators decided to turn to hypnosis. The witness

spoke and understood only Spanish, so it was Millie Markman again to the rescue.

Dolores was filthy from head to toe when she was first taken into custody for questioning. When two of the investigators on the case brought her to my office to meet me and Millie, she had been cleaned up and she was straight.

The young addict had never heard of hypnosis, much less experienced its effects. In Spanish, Millie described what was about to take place. She explained that there was nothing to fear, that the procedure was simply a means of helping people remember better. Dolores assured Millie that she understood. She said that she was not only ready and willing, but eager to give it a try.

The neophyte hypnotist put the woman under in short order. She gently eased her back to the day of the crime and asked her to describe what happened. Dolores' story deviated from what she had told the investigators only in the fact that she said she would have gone back to the apartment to see what she could do for Elena and Victor, if there had been the slightest chance of accomplishing anything by herself. In desperation, she hailed a man in a passing car and pleaded with him for help. He ignored her and drove on. It wasn't until then that the frightened woman ran to the subway.

When Millie asked Dolores what the men who got out of the cars looked like, the woman came up with some decent descriptions, and a few names. I noticed the investigators glance at each other wide-eyed when they heard the latter. They stood out amid the otherwise incomprehensible Spanish, and the men seemed to recognize them. Dolores was also more specific about the cars themselves. She said one was a limousine, and the other was a red Mustang with black louvers over the rear window.

After Millie had returned the young woman to an alert state, the investigators congratulated the officer on a job well done. They said the names that surfaced did indeed belong to characters known to be notorious members of the narcotics underworld and logical suspects in the killings.

Millie was thrilled. She glowed with the same feeling of triumph that comes over me every time hypnosis ferrets out the unknown from one of my subjects. I couldn't have been happier for her.

Three days later, the bubble burst. One of the detectives called and revealed that everything Dolores had told us about her whereabouts at the time of the crime was a lie. On the morning after her hypnotic interview, she broke down and admitted that, not only had she been in the apartment during the melee, she herself had taken part in it by personally slicing a throat or two. The investigator had yet to determine if Dolores had willingly conspired with the assailants to set a trap for the Guzmans, or if she had simply been forced to get her hands dirty in exchange for her own life. In any event, he credited hypnosis with the witness' change of heart. He thought the interview had helped her see the futility of sticking to her falsified alibi. He pointed out that, during the trance, she had already begun allowing herself to let some of the truth slip out; it was more than likely that the people she described and named really were the killers.

When advised of this development, Millie said she had had a feeling, during the interview, that Dolores knew more than she was letting on. But neither of us had really given much thought to whether or not the witness was telling the truth. This is up to the investigators. It is their job to corroborate. The fact that the subject was lying simply bears out the contention that people under hypnosis can fabricate as much as they please. A trance cannot compel them to speak only the truth, and if an investigator wants a ready means of separating fact from fiction in a deposition, he should seek the help of a lie detector, not hypnosis.

Millie's excellent work on the Guzman and Chen cases fueled my determination to get her transferred to the program. I wrote a formal request to Chief Sullivan and loaded it with ammunition. The fact that hypnosis would have contributed nothing to the two important homicide investigations without her efforts, plus her indispensability in handling Hispanics and sensitive rape situations evidently hit home. The chief gave in. He made a call to Millie's commander, Chief Voelker, and on January of 1980, she joined me on a permanent basis.

Aside from her invaluable assistance as an able-bodied hypnotist, the personable officer's presence has been especially helpful in defusing subjects' fears. If verbal assurances fail to convince a witness or victim of the harmlessness of hypnosis, I put Millie into a trance and ask the individual to talk to her and touch her while she is under. A cautious little tap or squeeze is usually followed by, "Did you feel that?" When Millie smiles and answers, "Yes, I felt it," it is more than evident she isn't in some drastically altered state. Sometimes I have the hypnosis candidate say the words that will "awaken" Millie. In most cases, once the witness sees how quickly and easily his suggestion returns the officer to her normally animated and cheerful self, he loses all anxiety, and is ready to experience the phenomenon himself. The technique is especially helpful with children.

In addition to the sessions I delegate to Millie, she routinely observes my interviews and participates in all the preliminaries. Before each session, with the witness out of the room, the detective tells us both, in general terms, what he would like to get from the interview—a description, a name, a license number, and so on. If he has a hunch about a particular suspect, I make sure he doesn't describe him. Or if the witness had already named a plate number, for instance, I don't want to know specifically what it is.

Another vital preliminary is a warning to the detective not to say anything during the interview, with the suggestion that, if he has a question, he should write it down and pass it to me. Toward the end of the session, I assure him, I will ask if he has any final queries before I bring the subject out of his trance. Some forensic hypnotists prefer to interview the witness without the detective in the room. But I like to have him there, so long as he abides by my guidelines. The witness might say something significant that should be pursued, and operating with as little familiarity with the investigation as possible, I might easily pass over the information in the investigator's absence.

Last, but far from least important among the preliminaries that deserve mention here is determining whether or not the witness is taking medication of any kind, or if he is under the ongoing care of a medical doctor or psychologist. If either is the case, I make sure I call the witness' doctor and tell him what we intend to do. If the doctor should say he doesn't want us to hypnotize his patient, we won't do it. So far, every physician and therapist

I have spoken to has allowed his patient to go ahead with the procedure, once I have explained how we work and what our credentials are.

Millie is now well versed in the preliminaries and precautions of forensic hypnosis. She has become a highly skilled practitioner, and her work was given deserved recognition recently when she was promoted to the rank of Detective. It is a good feeling to know that, if I retired tomorrow, I would be leaving the unit in able hands.

9

A LIFE RENEWED

Lisa Halloran was expecting her husband, his business partner, and the firm's newest client for dinner. The self-possessed forty-three-year-old suburbanite was confident that everything would be in order by the time they arrived. With her usual efficiency, she had worked all afternoon, making certain the evening would meet her husband Howard's exacting standards—the bar well stocked, with plenty of ice on hand, candles and fresh flowers on the table, and crudités with a dill and sour cream dip to serve with drinks. Dinner would be one of Howard's favorites: mushroom-capped filet mignon, broiled to just the right medium-rare pink, green beans and escalloped potatoes, followed by a crisp salad and Camembert at the perfect stage of ripeness—all with a good, but unpretentious Beaujolais Villages. Dessert would be Lisa's own famous cream cheese and cherry pie, always sure to draw raves, even from the most discriminating pastry fanciers.

Howard and his partner had started their own public relations company with a single client fifteen years ago. Now it serviced an impressive list of blue-chip accounts, and had a reputation as one of the best of New York's small, innovative agencies. Coming to dinner this evening was the president of a large midwest company specializing in gardening equipment. Howard's ingenious publicity and image-building ideas had spirited the client away from a rival public relations firm. The chief executive had never met Lisa, and Howard intended, with the invitation to his home, to impress the man with his discriminating taste in women and food.

Lisa, too, at one time had been a young executive on the rise. But she gave up a career of her own in favor of helping her husband establish his business and fulfilling his image of the perfect wife. And as far as Howard was concerned, she had done a smashing job. She was always there, looking radiantly attractive, whenever he needed her. There was just one small chink in the armor: Lisa had a drinking problem.

No one, least of all Howard, thought of Lisa as an alcoholic, though by definition, the label might be apt. It was just that whenever she had more than her usual two or three drinks at social functions, her personality made an abrupt about-face. She became nasty and abusive, and on more than one occasion, roundly offended friends of long standing. But to Lisa, the problem hardly existed. It was certainly nothing she couldn't handle. She would just make sure she cut herself off after two drinks before dinner, and everything would be fine.

The men were scheduled to arrive at seven. At six-thirty, Lisa was dressed and ready. The couple she had engaged to serve the food and drink were already there and busy with preparations. She had nothing to do but wait. The thought of pleasing Howard's client at all costs made her a little tense.

"I think I'll have my first drink now," she mused. "No harm in that. It'll calm me down, and then I'll nurse a second with the men before dinner."

When the three arrived at a little past seven, Lisa had one martini under her belt. She was feeling calm and self-assured, and got on famously with her husband's client. She was having such a good time, in fact, that her self-imposed alcoholic curfew went completely out of her head. As Howard watched with increasing concern and dismay, Lisa downed one drink after another. By the time the foursome got up to go to the table, she had had a total of five martinis and was swaying noticeably.

All would not have been lost if Lisa had stopped at that point. The meal would have sobered her enough to get her through the evening in decent shape. But too much wine and too little food during dinner was just the impetus she needed to send her tumbling over the edge.

It started with, "What did you say your company makes? String line trimmers? I think you need to use one on your hair. And that suit! You look like a hick from the hills." And continued on and off for a half-hour until Howard's client had had his fill. He asked Howard's partner to drive him back to the city, politely excused himself from the table, and walked out of the house.

Howard was furious. He swore to Lisa that, if he lost the account, he would not speak to her until she did something about her drinking. Either she could discipline herself, as she always said, or she couldn't. And if she couldn't, then she had better get some professional help.

Howard lost the account. Lisa was mortified. She realized now that she needed help, but didn't know who to turn to. She remembered a friend who had tried everything to stop overeating and lose weight. She succeeded only after being hypnotized. Lisa wondered if hypnosis could work as well with overdrinking. The friend gave her the number of the Babylon Hypnosis Center, and told her to speak to Charles Diggett.

The Babylon Hypnosis Center is the name I chose in 1975 for a private practice in hypnosis at my home in Babylon, Long Island. It originated as a means of accommodating requests for the therapeutic application of hypnosis and, at the same time, satisfying my own fascination with this aspect of the medium. In the hours outside tours of duty for the department, I have helped people lose weight, stop smoking, alleviate pain, improve athletic and academic performance, and overcome phobias.

In my phone conversation with Lisa, I explained that I had had experience working with four cases of alcoholism. In only one, unfortunately, had hypnosis been successful in curing the subject of the habit, and this person was purely a weekend alcoholic. From Monday to Friday, he was stone sober. I told Lisa that, of all the problems hypnosis can help people solve, alcoholism seemed to be the toughest nut to crack. Some hypnotherapists won't even see alcoholics for that very reason. I made sure she understood that hypnosis can help people only if they have really made up their mind that they want to achieve their goal, whatever it may be. She had to be determined to curtail her drinking or I couldn't help her.

To make the point, I described what happened with one of the problem drinkers who sought my help. A well-educated, successful man, he showed up for our first session inebriated. I told him there was no point in going ahead with the hypnosis. We wouldn't accomplish anything as long as he was drunk. We set up another appointment, and I sent him home. The next time he came, he was drunk again, and I sent him home again. This went on repeatedly until the guy gave up. Never showing up sober was his way of avoiding treatment. He still wanted to drink, and was far from ready to make a commitment to stop.

Lisa made it clear that she was willing, at this point, to take whatever steps were necessary to overcome her problem. I told her I would be glad to see what I could do. We set up an appointment for the following evening.

The woman was an excellent subject. She went into a hypnotic trance of medium depth, neither of us exerting any special effort. When she was ready, I began the exercise I had chosen for her specific need, one I felt had the best chance of success.

"I want you to visualize a row of lights in your mind's eye, Lisa. Imagine that they're in an assortment of colors and that each one is hooked up to a different part of your body. Can you see the lights?"

"Yes, I can."

"Good. I'd like you to pick out the light that controls your right arm. Do you know which one it is?"

"Yes."

"What color is it?"

"Blue."

"Okay, fine. Imagine that you reach up and turn that blue light off. When you do, you'll turn off all the nerves to your right arm. You won't be able to feel anything in it. It'll be numb, as though it didn't belong to you. As soon as you've turned the light off, raise your left hand."

Lisa concentrated for a moment, and then her left hand went up. To be sure she had accepted the suggestion, I pinched her right hand a few times. There was no reaction. I asked if she felt anything, and she said no, she didn't.

I was glad the exercise was one Lisa could respond to. Described in a number of books, it is a well-known technique for turning off pain in a specific body part. I went ahead with the adaptation of it I had devised to deal with Lisa's problem.

"Turn the blue light back on now, Lisa. That'll restore feeling to your right arm. . . . Does it feel as if it's normal again?"

"Yes, it does."

"Good. This time, I want you to look at the red light. Can you see a red light among the colored lights in your mind?"

"Yes."

"From now on, whenever you've had your second drink at a social function, or wherever you might be, that red light will go on. And when it does, alcoholic beverages will taste awful to you. But non-alcoholic liquids will taste better than they ever have. You'll enjoy soft drinks and juices, things you may never have liked before."

When I was certain the suggestion had penetrated the recesses of Lisa's mind, I returned her to consciousness. I showed her how to hypnotize herself with the eye-roll method, and told her to use it whenever the red light needed reinforcement. Just before she left, she told me she would be attending a party in a few days, and would be looking forward to seeing if the post-hypnotic suggestion had taken. I, too, was anxious to find out whether or not the technique selected was a good one for this particular situation.

A week later, Lisa called, breathless with excitement. She praised me as a miracle worker. "Just as you said," she exclaimed, "I was about to sip my third drink, when I saw that red warning light. I took a gulp just the same, and it was the worst thing I ever tasted. I almost had to spit it out. I switched to mineral water, and I never enjoyed it so much. I was really amazed."

Four months later, Lisa called again. She just wanted to let me know that she was still in control of her drinking. "That little red light is the best friend I ever had. Howard is very proud of me."

I haven't heard from Lisa since, and I presume it is because she needs no further help. When hypnosis is successful with a long shot like Lisa's triumph over addiction, nobody is more pleased and surprised than I am.

Arthur Hansen was a partner in the architecture firm, Marshall and Hansen. Although he owned half the business, and was an accomplished professional architect, he lacked the one thing that would earn him the right to the title officially: a license.

The examination always got the better of him. He had failed it four times, and his partner, Bill Marshall, was becoming more and more annoyed with him. He and Bill had been awarded degrees by the same school at the same time, and Bill had gotten his license years ago.

Arthur was scheduled to take the test again. He was involved in the by-now familiar ritual of boning up on all the technicalities he would be required to know, when his wife came across an article about me in *People* magazine. The story mentioned my using hypnosis on my wife to help her pass her driver's test, and the architect's wife pointed this out, suggesting he consider hypnosis to help him with his own seemingly insurmountable problem.

Arthur hadn't the slightest faith in the medium, and couldn't imagine it making a difference when so much effort and concentration had failed him in the past. But to please his wife and because he was convinced he had nothing to lose, he came to see me.

At the root of the architect's difficulty was the classic test-anxiety syndrome. It was obvious that he had more than enough knowledge and experience to be able to answer the questions on the examination correctly. But his lack of confidence was so great, it did him in. Each time he took the test, the pressure to pass increased, and with it, the anxiety that defeated him. The self-perpetuating cycle had to be broken.

And it was. In three separate sessions in the weeks before the test, I gave Arthur hypnotic suggestions of confidence and relaxation, and assurance that he had all the knowledge and ability he needed to be a licensed architect. I instructed him in self-hypnosis, and told him to use it during the examination if he felt the slightest trace of anxiety.

Arthur passed the test. At the victory party he threw for himself, he was jubilant. "You know, Charlie, never in all the times I've taken that damn test did I feel as self-assured and together as I did the other day. My head was humming along like a computer. I'll never be skeptical about hypnosis again."

Patricia Delaney loved tennis. A vigorous woman in her early fifties, she had won a well-deserved reputation on the amateur circuits playing against women much younger than herself. But like most dedicated athletes, she was always on the lookout for ways to improve her game. In the course of her travels, she met players who claimed to have made substantial gains with the help of hypnosis.

Not to be outdone, Pat looked me up. She wanted to know if it was true that if she were hypnotized, she would become a better player. I told her this depended on a number of contingencies, but yes, I had helped some people improve their performance, and the only way she could really find out if it would work for her would be to try.

Pat took to hypnosis with the greatest of ease. She knew how to focus her energies. She had to to hold her own in tennis. Her absolute determination to make the therapy effective was another giant step in her favor. Her faith in the medium virtually predetermined its success.

The technique I used is one that has gained popular acceptance among therapists for athletic endeavors of all kinds, or for that matter, any physical activity requiring a degree of skill. It demands intense visualization, which most hypnotic subjects seem able to achieve. Pat scored high on the induction profile, so I was optimistic that she would get the results she expected.

While the subject was in a deep trance, I suggested, "See

yourself playing the perfect game in slow motion. Watch every move. You've never in your life performed so well. You make no mistakes whatsoever. You feel the pleasurable sensation of your body responding beautifully, in absolute harmony with your mind. Your forehand is perfect. Your backhand is perfect. You anticipate and meet every one of your opponent's challenges. You can do no wrong. You're invincible. . . ."

When I was convinced the cheering-section abetments had gotten through to Pat, and she was truly bringing them to life in her mind, I implanted a post-hypnotic suggestion: "Before every game, you'll go through the same process of envisioning a fault-less performance. But when you're actually playing, you won't think about that at all. You'll just be very relaxed, and what you experienced under hypnosis will be implemented automatically. It'll become a conditioned reflex."

The hypnotherapy worked so well for Pat that she went on to win the championship in her league. But the success made her eager for more. She wanted to move up to a more competitive level, so she came to see me again.

I was concerned at this point that, in pitting herself against ever younger and faster opponents, Pat was in danger of being taxed beyond her physical resources. I worried about the possibility of a heart attack, and told her I wouldn't hypnotize her again until she had cleared it with her doctor.

I got word from Pat's physician that the woman was in remarkable physical shape for her age and that there would be no harm in allowing her to improve her game further through hypnosis. Pat and I had one more session a few months ago, and I haven't heard anything from her since. But I have every confidence that she is burning up the courts and piling one victory on top of another.

Richard Mitchell was a basketball pro with a serious problem. It didn't have anything to do with his game. That was fine. What Richard was having difficulty with was the constant travel from one tournament to another. If he could have made the trips by train or bus, he wouldn't have had anything to worry about. But his team's schedule demanded the speed and convenience of air travel, and Richard had a terrible fear of flying.

The young man came to see me in the hopes of curing his phobia. He brought his wife Gloria along, and before I attempted to hypnotize Richard, the three of us chatted for a while. The athlete described the awful fear that all but paralyzed him for the duration of any flight. The severe anxiety had become intolerable, and he was going to have to give up basketball if he couldn't learn to overcome it. Gloria confirmed the urgency of the situation.

When the conversation was over, I was left with the distinct impression that Richard had reached the point where he was no longer interested in a career in basketball, that he was continuing only because it meant a great deal to his wife. After Gloria had left the room to allow me to devote my attention to the subject in private, I asked Richard if there was any truth to the observation.

"Oh no," he replied, "I love being a professional athlete and wouldn't dream of giving it up."

I wasn't convinced. Nonetheless, I decided to go ahead with the hypnosis and see if I could help Richard come to terms with his irrational fear.

He was not among the most susceptible hypnotic subjects. After a number of failed attempts, I finally succeeded in coaxing him into a light trance. The suggestions I gave him included positive reinforcement concerning the relative safety of air travel and the groundlessness of his anxiety. I also told him, "Just being in a plane will give you a feeling of warmth and coziness. The sound of the engines will have a calming effect."

After showing Richard how to hypnotize himself, I advised him to go into a trance every time he was about to take a flight —at home, at the airport, wherever he could steal a quiet moment—and to suggest to himself that there was nothing to be afraid of, that he would be relaxed, comfortable, and confident all the while he was aboard the plane. I recommended he repeat the process in his seat or in the lavatory, if he felt the slightest twinge of nervousness while in the air.

Actually, I doubted that Richard would be able to achieve a state of hypnosis on his own, given his low level of suggestibility, so I urged him, "If you're unable to go into a trance, just try to become as relaxed as you can, and then make the same suggestions to yourself."

A few weeks later, Gloria called to tell me the hypnosis had been successful. "For the first time in years," she said, "Richard can cope with flying. He says the suggestions he makes to himself really work. The funny thing, though, is now his game is off. He's not playing nearly as well as he used to."

If my hunch about Richard's not wanting to continue his career was correct—and I think it was—this development was understandable. The manifestation of the athlete's reluctance simply had been transferred from fear of flying to not playing well. Hypnosis could just as well have helped him with his new problem and improved his game, but the discontent at the root of it all would have surfaced somewhere else. Hypnotherapy can alter undesirable behavior patterns, but it can also uncover deep-seated wishes and frustrations that must be resolved before the subject can find true relief. The best analogy that comes to mind is the treatment of a bodily disease. The patient can be relieved of its symptoms, but if it isn't cured, it will continue to cause him problems.

The case histories described here represent just a small sampling of the many people I have had the opportunity to help modify behavior of one kind or another. Because I have always loved and been fascinated by people, and have great admiration for the human spirit, my hypnotherapy practice is a source of tremendous self-gratification.

I don't mean to minimize the financial rewards either. While the amount of money derived from the endeavor is rather small, these days, every nickel and dime helps. An extra fifty dollars here and there solved the problem of where I would get the money to buy my son a pair of shoes for his graduation, and has bailed me out on more than one occasion in my efforts to keep a family-of-six economic ship afloat. But much more satisfying than monetary gain is the happiness and sense of fulfillment I experience when someone calls or writes to tell me he is feeling much better or has accomplished something he never could before because of the few conversations we had. This kind of feedback can hardly be measured in dollars and cents.

It seems that the longer I practice hypnotherapy, the more surprised and amazed I am at the extent to which an individual's quality of life can be improved by the simple verbal exchange we call hypnosis. When beginning a session with someone who is interested in losing weight, for example, or quitting cigarettes—and 90 per cent of the people who come to me are seeking help in these two areas—I am almost always tempted to think, "This isn't going to work. It's ridiculous. I'm wasting my time and his. How can I expect the few words I say to reverse a lifetime of habitual indulgence?" But I suppose I am a habitual doubting Thomas—a problem of mine to tackle under self-hypnosis? Yes, because I know by now that, more often than not, the person will call and announce proudly, "I haven't smoked in three weeks," or, "I've lost twelve pounds." People and what they can accomplish renew my faith every time.

In a forensic hypnotic context, the situation is the same. Insecurities about being able to refresh a witness' memory are a part of every interview. When the subject reveals details even he wasn't aware of before, I am amazed, yet still skeptical. But in this case, my doubts are in the best interests of the situation. They serve to strengthen my warnings to the investigators that the witness' remarks are not to be accepted as fact, that corroborative evidence must be found. If the investigators tell me later that what hypnosis uncovered was indeed factual information, then I am more amazed than ever. Just convincing a person that he will be better able to recall, once he is relaxed, which is all I do, seems too innocuous an undertaking for the results it garners.

Likewise, if hypnotherapy does no more than instill subjects with the conviction that they have within themselves the resources to conquer their fears and phobias or achieve more than they ever have before, the results can be astounding. Let me offer an example. A few years ago and before he knew me, a friend of mine visited a hypnotherapist in search of a means of giving up cigarettes. He had stopped smoking only to start up again many times before that. He told me, "I saw this guy just once, and all he did was talk to me for a few minutes from behind his desk while I sat opposite him. As far as I could tell, he didn't hypnotize me in any way, and I left his office thinking he was a real quack. I felt cheated. Then, while I was waiting for the bus outside his office, for no reason at all and without really thinking about it, I took the pack of cigarettes I had with me out of my pocket and threw it into a nearby trash bin. That was three years ago, and I haven't smoked a single cigarette since!"

Although no formal induction was involved, my friend was obviously in the hands of an excellent therapist, if even for a few minutes. What happened was, the practitioner was able to relax the smoker to the point that his own suggestions of the harm he was doing to his body and of the power he himself held to control his own destiny were accepted by his subconscious so deeply and completely that they reprogrammed his behavior automatically.

My occasional lack of trust in its efficacy notwithstanding, hypnotic therapy is a powerful force that can also be a dangerous one in the hands of untrained or irresponsible operators. One area in which the point is well made is that of the treatment of pain. Releasing people from its unremitting bondage is within the grasp of hypnosis. But pain is the body's means of alerting us to the fact that something is wrong, and if the therapist doesn't take this into account, he can provide relief for his subject at the expense of the medical attention the individual may be in dire need of.

If someone comes to me seeking relief from an intractable headache, for example, the first thing I want to know is whether or not the individual has seen a doctor about it. If not, I explain that I will not perform the hypnosis unless and until he has done so. If he says he has been treated by a doctor, I provide him with one of the forms I have drawn up for this purpose, and ask him to have his doctor fill it out. The form tells the physician that his patient has sought relief from head pain through hypnotherapy, and asks him if he has any objections, recommendations, or special instructions regarding the course of treatment. The doctor may forbid hypnotherapy, in which case I go no further. He may say, "Fine, go ahead. I trust your judgment," or he may have in mind a particular procedure he would like me to follow. In any case, once I have the physician's approval, I proceed with the hypnotic treatment, but all along the way, I keep in touch with him, letting him know how his patient is reacting and making sure he has no reservations about what is going on.

The life-disrupting, unyielding pain of such disorders as arthritis, tension or migraine headaches or the discomfort caused by injury or surgery all can be removed or lessened by means of hypnosis. And the danger of "masking" an indication of a more serious malady is minimal in such instances. Yet, before attempting to alleviate *any* pain, a therapist must be absolutely certain as to its source, and this is why communication between the hypnotic practitioner and the subject's physician is vital. Intermittent tension headaches may seem innocuous enough, but if the pain is a symptom of high blood pressure, eye strain, or even a brain tumor in an early stage of development, it would certainly be foolhardy to have it alleviated by hypnosis and then dismiss it without ever seeing a doctor.

Incredible as it may seem, extraordinarily suggestible subjects can be hypnotized to withstand surgery without an anesthetic. The procedure has been attempted only in the most extreme circumstances, such as for a patient requiring emergency surgery when he is unable to tolerate any kind of pain-killing or soporific drug. As rare as it is, the example of ultimate pain-deadening defines hypnosis' almost unlimited potential.

Some months before my oldest son Dennis' wife Peggy was due to deliver her first child, at her request, I began a series of hypnotherapy sessions, suggesting that the delivery would be as smooth and effortless as possible, with minimum discomfort. To prepare for the coming event, Peggy became adept at putting herself into a trance with little effort. Our scheme was attempted only with the approval and participation of her obstetrician, and we all succeeded beyond our fondest hopes. Peggy gave birth almost totally without pain and was able to enjoy the experience to the fullest.

Probably because hypnosis is an effective pain remedy, it has been suggested that healing and curative powers are among its capabilities. Although it wouldn't surprise me in the least if this were found to be so some time in the future, I have yet to see any evidence of it. Unless, of course, I take into account those bodily afflictions rooted in mental stress and strain—ulcers and perhaps asthma, among others. While hypnosis cannot directly cure these disorders, it can offset the disruptive mental forces that give rise to them.

In hypnotic treatment, a sufferer is given the suggestion that he remain calm and relaxed in the face of the circumstances he finds disturbing. Once he is able to deal more positively with the source of his anxiety, whether it be a stressful situation at work, financial difficulties, or an overbearing mother-in-law, it will no longer threaten his physical health. If he already suffers from an illness directly traceable to emotional strain, the condition will certainly be relieved, if not cured.

One of the proposals to come out of the great body of cancer research recently is that the menacing aberrant cells flourish because the mind, for some reason, either slows or completely shuts down the normal activity of the body's immune system. The process operates on an involuntary level of the brain. In other words, like heart rate, blood pressure, metabolic activity, we have no conscious control over it. Just why the brain turns off the life-protecting system is not yet known, although it has been suggested that it may have something to do with a depressed emotional state or a subconscious wish for self-destruction, denial, or punishment. At any rate, the therapy being developed in response to the speculation includes psychological counseling to try to reverse the mind's negative point of view. But more telling, as far as hypnosis is concerned, is the fact that patients are being urged to seek moments of quiet and relaxation and to concentrate on envisioning their antibodies attacking and killing their cancer cells. One person told me he likes to imagine his antibodies are little soldiers with automatic rifles, slaying enemy cells one by one.

The point is, the mental exercise is obviously an attempt at self-hypnosis. Though the term is never mentioned in this particular therapy, it is good to see that the medical establishment is gradually coming around to the realization of how much the health of the body is dependent on the emotional stability and well-being of the mind. Even more encouraging is the fact that having patients fix on marshaling their body's immunity resources shows signs, in some cases, of working. The approach actually may be an effective means of fighting cancer, although it is still too early for any conclusive evidence.

I mentioned we have no conscious control over many of the body's vital functions. But if research into the workings of the mind continues at its present rate, we may eventually discover that human beings can manipulate at will much of what we always thought of as involuntary. What other explanation can there be for the Buddhist masters who subsist for months without eating, or survive for hours in air-tight chambers, their oxygen supply severely reduced? These enlightened Eastern philosophers have developed a kind of control over their bodies that most of humanity has yet to dream of. They can order their heart and respiration rates to slow, thereby reducing the activity of all the body's systems to the point that only minuscule amounts of oxygen and food are necessary to keep them functioning efficiently. If you ask the mystics how they do it, they will say meditation. But meditation, yoga, auto-hypnosis—to me, it is the same loaf of bread sliced a little differently.

Away from the ashrams, in the more conservative halls of cautious Western scientific experimentation, the term hypnosis is being uttered without apology with greater frequency. A recent television report on medical technology frontiers took viewers into a laboratory where a young woman had been taught to control her own blood pressure through hypnosis. Paralyzed since childhood, the woman had remained prone for so many years that whenever a sitting position was attempted, blood pressure in her brain dropped so drastically that she passed out. To overcome the problem, she suggested to herself, under hypnosis, that her blood would maintain pressure when her upper body was raised. After a great deal of practice, she succeeded, and now has no problem sitting up for short periods.

The graphic television image of that blood pressure indicator plummeting every time the woman's head was raised, and then miraculously remaining stable after she had hypnotized herself, is one I will always remember. It brought home the point that hypnosis' potential to erase the distinction between voluntary and involuntary systems was no longer an empty claim or the province of mystics, but was already being demonstrated scientifically.

Almost as life-crippling as physical disability are the many phobias that can plague the human psyche. It's impossible for victims of claustrophobia, to name one, to lead normal lives—not when the mere thought of entering an elevator, a windowless room, or even a car or bus sends the heart racing, palms sweating, knees buckling. Concessions and adjustments must be made constantly to avoid the dreaded enclosed confinement. The opposite of this affliction, agoraphobia (literally, "fear of the marketplace"), condemns its sufferers to life imprisonment in their own homes. These unfortunates wouldn't dream of walking a block to buy a quart of milk, much less stroll in a park, visit a department store, or see a movie. It is difficult, if not impossible, for anyone free of phobias to appreciate fully the altered behavior and ways of life they demand.

Yet victims need not remain entrapped. Hypnotherapy can set them free. I have been privileged to help a handful of people throw off the disturbing shackles of phobic response. But the hypnotic treatment can be painstaking, at times requiring numerous sessions over an extended period. Eventually, full recovery is achieved in some cases, with lives affected far more dramatically than in any other area of hypnotic therapy. When rescued phobia sufferers report being able to use an elevator or go outdoors for the first time in years, my heart swells with pride and gratitude, and my mind is in awe of the medium that restored them to full and happy lives.

Among other disabling phenomena of the mind I have had the experience of treating are both insomnia and its converse, inopportune drowsiness. Whether the latter is caused by going too many hours without food, early-morning sluggishness, or a late-afternoon slump, it is not all that disturbing, and can be reversed quickly with a brief self-hypnotic suggestion. But sleep tendency in the extreme, called narcolepsy, is a condition that can be life-disrupting, to say the least. Its victims, no matter where they are or what they are doing, drop off to sleep abruptly for no apparent reason. Although I have never encountered the disease in my hypnotic practice, I suspect it would respond to the therapy—of course, demanding more intense treatment than related mild drowsiness.

I rely on hypnosis, myself, as a pick-me-up, which I seem to need more often than I would like. In fact, self-hypnosis on the Long Island Railroad has become almost a daily ritual. When I board the train in the morning, I am usually feeling fine, ready for a day of work. But during the trip, I barely make it halfway through the paper when I begin dozing off. By the time the train is fifteen minutes out of Penn Station, I rouse myself, but I am really dragging. That is when I go into hypnosis via the eye-roll induction. So as not to give the other passengers the impression that there is an asylum escapee in their midst, though, I close my eyes before I roll them up, rather than after. This doesn't seem to affect my ability to go into a trance. While I am under, I suggest to myself, "In ten seconds, I'm going to count from three to one. When I get to one, I'll be wide awake, full of vim, vigor, and vitality and ready to go." Normally, this does the trick, unless I am really exhausted, maybe because of fitful sleep for two or three nights in a row. In that case, my body seems to say, "The hell with you, I'm not going to respond," and the suggestions of alertness don't work.

Hypnosis has its limits, but this little exercise is usually effective and one anyone can do any time of the day when his or her energy level falls below optimum.

In situations of insomnia, however, it certainly would not make sense to suggest to oneself, "When I get to one, I'll feel alert, and then I'll begin falling asleep." The two conflicting suggestions equal one very self-defeating approach that would likely aggravate the situation, and make sleep even more difficult.

Most of the insomniacs I have treated have trouble falling asleep because they can't seem to get their minds to shut down. While lying in bed, their heads race with the day's worries and problems, and the more they *try* to sleep, the more active their minds become. The best hypnotic techniques for insomnia are calculated to distract subjects from trying, while beguiling them to keep letting go until overcome by a state of reverie. My favorite exercise for inducing sleep has proven effective time and again.

After I have shown a subject how to hypnotize himself, I advise him, "While lying comfortably in bed, try not to think at all about sleep. Just go into hypnosis as you've done here, and then say to yourself, 'Now I'm going to count backward from a hundred to one. With every count, I'll become more and more relaxed.' Don't say anything about falling asleep. Then go ahead and begin the count. Breathe slowly, as you do while sleeping, and take one breath with each count. Say the word 'deeper' to yourself after every number, and just concentrate on letting your body go and on becoming more and more relaxed each time you repeat 'deeper.' More than likely, you'll doze off long before you reach the count of one."

The process is reminiscent of the old stand-by, those ubiquitous little sheep hopping over fences, which, when it works, is actually a form of hypnosis. The traditional sleep inducer just needed to be improved a little by modern hypnotic know-how.

In addition to physical pains and ills, fears, phobias, insomnia, and athletic prowess, hypnotherapy is a viable means of bettering professional performance of all kinds. There isn't a single manual, intellectual, or creative skill, whether it be typing, accounting, plumbing, carpentry, painting, sculpting, personnel management, salesmanship, that cannot be improved through hypnosis. The therapy even helps conquer the bane of authors, writer's block. One of my most satisfying cases, as a matter of fact, involved a screenwriter for whom the terror of the empty page almost spelled the end of a career.

The man was in the middle of composing the screenplay for a major motion picture when he reached an impasse. The deadline he had committed himself to was only weeks away, so he was under great pressure to get back to work and finish the project. A friend of his familiar with my efforts sent him to see me.

Most writers have a well-developed sense of imagination, an indication of hypnotic susceptibility, and this one was no exception. He was a good subject and quickly learned how to hypnotize himself. The strategy I recommended to overcome his current creative block and any future problems involved going into hypnosis right at the typewriter and imagining that he was sitting in a theater about to watch a film. "Suggest to yourself that the film you're going to see," I said to him, "and the characters in it are what you've created and are now working on. As the film begins to roll, just sit back, relax, and allow the people to behave, speak, and interact as they please. Then, when you think you've seen enough, come out of hypnosis and write what transpired. Actually, the visualized performance is no more than the workings of your own imagination, the hypnotic device merely being a means of freeing your own innate creative powers of all inhibiting or distracting influences."

The technique is applicable to creating all forms of fiction. For authors wishing help with the non-fiction format, however, the visualization approach is only occasionally appropriate. To overcome a frustrating loss of words in writing of this kind, I would advise subjects to suggest to themselves that they will make their minds blank, that they are not going to think about anything and will be as quiet and reposed as possible, that in a short while, the flow of words they are after will come to them. Then, if they really relax, allow themselves to become a part of the chair they are sitting in, the concept or expression they have been struggling for will surface without any strain.

The screenwriter called a few weeks later and reported, "Charlie, it worked like a dream. I never would've believed it, but those characters said things and acted in ways I know I couldn't have thought of without going into hypnosis. The screenplay is finished, and everybody's saying it's the best thing I've ever done."

The remarkable and varied techniques I have appropriated over the years are the real heroes to be credited with the staggering accomplishments of many of the people I have hypnotized. The ingenious exercises are the brain children of behavioral scientists who have devoted their lives to the study of the phenomenon of hypnosis. What led Dr. Herbert Spiegel, the psychiatrist and well-known hypnotic authority, for example, to conclude that the key to being hypnotized lay in the peculiar signal of upward-rolling eyes? Keeping his own eyes level and open was what put him on the trail of a technique that became the doorway to hypnosis for many.

By carefully observing the reactions of the thousands of people he has hypnotized over the years, the Columbia professor noted that when many of these subjects went into a trance, no matter what the induction procedure, their eyes rolled up without prompting. The move could be seen even behind the lids of those whose eyes were closed beforehand. People also will frequently roll their eyes just before fainting, or when searching for a lost memory or the answer to a difficult question. And in certain religious organizations, in the tradition of the "holy rollers," congregations are inspired to sway and chant until members work themselves into a "divine frenzy," baring the whites of their eyes and "speaking in unknown tongues"—an example of mass hypnosis, if not hysteria, in action.

After returning home from one of Dr. Spiegel's seminars at which the point was covered, I was sitting in the living room, and my dog was lying nearby. I just happened to look at him as he put his head down, rolled his eyes up, and, in an instant, went off to sleep. I remember thinking, "That's exactly what Spiegel was talking about!" Since then, I have seen other dogs nod off in the same quick way. I don't know for a fact that this is a further example of the doctor's observation, but I have a suspicion it is.

As a result of his research, the professor took the eye-roll response and turned it into an active means of helping subjects go under. He *asked* people to roll their eyes up, and a new method of induction was born. Actually, the precedent had already been set. A hypnotist by the name of David Ellman describes a similar technique in a book he wrote some years ago. Dr. Spiegel went one step further and concluded that anyone who wasn't able to accomplish the eye movement couldn't be hypnotized. I am not in 100 per cent agreement with him on this point, however. In my experience, subjects incapable of the maneuver cannot be hypnotized by the eye-roll induction. But this isn't to say that they won't go under by means of one of the various progressive-relaxation techniques available, if I spend the time and effort required. Yet there is little doubt that the correlation Dr. Spiegel discovered operates somewhere in the labyrinthine workings of the mind; those who aren't able to achieve the eye movement cannot be hypnotized as quickly or as deeply as those who can.

Another source of hypnotic procedures is the wellspring of techniques developed and used by psychotherapists to reverse undesirable behavior patterns or to restore peace of mind to the emotionally disturbed. Some are borrowed intact, while others are modified to suit the hypnotist or the situation. A good example is the split-screen technique I use in my investigative work to recover memories lost to the subconscious. The exercise was originally devised to help patients differentiate between acceptable and unacceptable behavior. On one side of the screen, the individual would imagine seeing himself dealing with a situation in a way that caused him frustration, anxiety, whatever. And on the other, he would be reacting to the same situation as he should have, in a much healthier fashion.

When exposed to the mental exercise, I immediately saw it as an excellent backup measure, to put into action when some of the less imaginative relaxation techniques failed to coax witnesses to remember. I simply adapted it so that one side of the screen revealed conscious memories, and forgotten details would make themselves known on the other.

Resourcefulness is as much the name of the game as confidence, experience, and training. Without it, I know I would have accomplished a lot less than I have in both the therapeutic and forensic arenas.

While many of the people I have hypnotized under investigative circumstances have been aware of my hypnotherapy practice, only once have these separate professional efforts been linked by a common recipient.

Just as Hilda Dorfman was falling asleep in her first-floor apartment in Brooklyn, she heard a noise at her bedroom window. When the elderly woman got up to investigate, she saw a man trying to break in. Taken by surprise, the vandal jumped to the sidewalk, and ran around the corner of the building. Hilda moved to another window, and saw the man pass by, as he raced down the street.

The woman had come face to face with the Flatbush Night Stalker, suspected at the time of having raped at least twenty-five women, all over fifty. Under hypnosis, the near victim gave us a good description of the rapist. The man was never found, but the assaults stopped abruptly and mysteriously, as if the fugitive had moved away or been arrested for an unrelated crime.

Hilda was so impressed by the hypnotic interview that she elected to have me help her lose weight through hypnotherapy. We had just one session together. I recommended more, but Hilda began shedding pounds immediately, and was confident that no further appointments were necessary. Some time later, her daughter called to tell me that her mother had slimmed down considerably, and was managing to stay on her diet.

People often ask me if they can expect to accomplish as much in a group-hypnosis setting as they would in a one-on-one situation. What they are referring to are the much-advertised hypnosis centers that are popping up everywhere with increasing frequency. Just how effective are these institutions in helping individuals reach their behavioral goals? The answer is, the best work for some, and the worst are to be avoided by all.

A scattering of these organizations is run by competent and respected members of the hypnotic community, and I have no doubt that these skilled practitioners have devised programs that have benefited many. And I wouldn't be surprised to find other group-hypnotherapy centers that are reliable sources of betterment in such areas as sports, studies, salesmanship, and perhaps giving up cigarettes and other undesirable habits. But if an institution proffers claims of relieving pain, curing phobias and physical ills, and there is no evidence anywhere of an advisory medical or psychological professional, it is definitely to be avoided.

Losing weight, also, is a far more hypnotically complicated situation than most hypnosis centers would have people believe. Being able to diet down to one's ideal weight is only the first half of the battle. The moment of truth lies in keeping the weight off. And this can be accomplished only when an individual is helped to understand the emotional factors that forged a lifetime of food-associated behavior. Because the psychological dynamics vary so from one person to another, no group-hypnosis effort can be expected to meet every subject's need.

On the whole, I can't help harboring a certain prejudice against the supermarket approach to hypnosis. I am of the opinion that the overriding priority of hypnosis-by-the-dozen is financial solvency rather than hypnotic effectiveness.

Let us say that a gathering of twenty people is hypnotized by one particular method, and each subject is given tapes to take home and listen to repeatedly. At so much per head, the center reaps a nice bit of change for very little time and effort. I wouldn't deny any organization their due profit, except that, in this case, the pursuit of quantity sacrifices quality. A generous estimate would be that maybe seven of the group of twenty will be successful in achieving their goals. But what about the other thirteen? They are out of luck, and might just as well throw their money away. The setting won't be effective for them because they happen not to be capable of responding to the particular technique they are being exposed to. They need an alternative.

This is why I prefer directing my efforts to one person at a time. It allows every individual the best possible chance of obtaining results, and the hypnotist the opportunity to see if his approach is working or not. If one procedure doesn't take, I can always switch to another until I find the strategy best suited to the subject's own special hypnotic disposition. There is no denying the fact that some people will benefit from group hypnosis, despite being herded with others. But the situation cannot possibly accommodate the unique abilities, inclinations, and associations of the minds of each member of the group.

The most outlandish offering openly advertised by apparently reputable hypnosis centers is the experience of reliving a previous life. The supposed journey of the mind backward in time is actually a common practice among some of the more progressive of my freethinking colleagues, who, no doubt, have been prompted by the proven hypnotic capability of regressing subjects to the earliest years of their present lives. There are even cases of people claiming to remember the trauma of birth, and still earlier, the prenatal warmth and darkness of the womb. Curious to know what, if anything, lay beyond conception, hypnotists regressed the extremely suggestible subjects further, and that is when they reported hitherto unknown lives, describing environments they had never been in, and speaking in languages they were unfamiliar with.

Is there life before conception? Adherents of the philosophy of reincarnation will say we have all lived hundreds, if not thousands, of lives, and have many more to look forward to. But none of the recognized hypnotic experts I have spoken to about this brand of regression would label it legitimate reliving of former lives. They all regard the subjects' descriptions, astounding as they may seem, as figments of the imagination, embellishments of hidden remembrances that are released by the deep hypnotic trance.

What about the fact that the subjects prattle on in languages they have no knowledge of in a non-hypnotic state? In almost every seriously investigated case, some exposure to the language, however brief, at some point in the subject's life, has been found. It might have been a snippet of a radio broadcast or a non-English-speaking domestic or governess overheard when the subject was far too young for the memory to exist on a conscious level in adulthood. That the language is regenerated faultlessly without effort, in itself, is pretty remarkable, but for the most susceptible subjects, total recall under hypnosis is not unusual.

Whether an individual believes the regression procedure to be a genuine doorway to the events and circumstances of a once-lived life or simply a means of tapping the limitless resources of his imagination, there is no harm in the experience if it is approached with a spirit of lightheartedness. In fact, he may benefit by it beyond satisfying his curiosity, if he happens to visit one hypnotherapist I know of.

This particular practitioner has an interesting way of relieving chronic pain, once he has ascertained that it is not an indication of serious dysfunction. If a woman comes to him with a non-symptomatic, recurring headache, for example, he will tell her something on the order of, "I'm going to hypnotize you and regress you to a previous life to see if we can find anything that would explain why you have these headaches." The woman now has been given the license to imagine whatever she would like. Under hypnosis, she might be surprised to find herself saying, "I'm aware that the time is around the turn of the century, and I'm wearing high-button shoes and a red satin dress. My God, I'm a dancer in a saloon in Dead Gulch, Arizona. There's a shoot-out, and a stray bullet catches me in the head and does me in!" The therapist can then point out to his subject that of course she has these recurring headaches. They are nagging remnants of her last life's violent demise. "Now that you know that," he'll say, "you should be able to realize that you have no need of the pain in this life. When I bring you out of hypnosis, you'll be totally free of the encumbrance, and will never have to endure it again."

The hypnotist has sworn that the strategy is sometimes successful. Whether or not the subject really did once serve a turn as a dance-hall girl, or ever lived another life at all, is beside the point. What matters is that the procedure provided a means for the woman to rid herself of needless pain, not to mention the fact that she will forever have a story she can count on to fascinate her friends.

Should all of us expect to be able to unleash spine-tingling adventures lived during fabled eras in exotic places, and be impeccably articulate in tongues we never could quite get the hang of in our school days? No, because this sort of hypnotic experience, whether imaginary or documented, demands a degree of susceptibility well beyond the average. The disposition to hypnosis is a talent, not unlike musical or artistic ability, and everyone has an in-born capacity to achieve a particular depth. The level varies with each of us, and as coldhearted as it may seem, it remains fixed for life. There is nothing we can do to alter it.

However, there are all kinds of influences and prevailing circumstances that get in the way of reaching our ultimate capacities, and we *can* exercise a degree of control over these interferences. One is fear. The only way to eliminate it is by repeated exposure to the hypnotic process, either as an observer or as a subject. The more opportunities you have of watching people being hypnotized in the flesh, the less apprehensive you are likely to be. You will see that nothing inordinate is involved, and will begin to understand that any anxiety at all is unreasonable. When *your* turn comes, you will be more relaxed and susceptible. This is the reason for demonstrating the process with the help of my assistant Millie before attempting to hypnotize a witness or victim I can tell is locked in the grip of fear.

The adage practice makes perfect is as appropriate for hypnosis as for any intellectual skill. The more often you are hypnotized, or attempt self-hypnosis, the easier it will be to go under, and the closer you will approach optimum depth. My conclusion in this respect differs from Dr. Spiegel's. He insists that just one session is required; whatever level the subject reaches is all he will ever be able to achieve. Other experts say that an individual won't attain full capacity until he or she has experienced at least seven or eight sessions. In yielding to study, hypnosis is still as elusive as the atom, and the decision of the hypnotic judges on this issue is as arbitrary as it is on assessment of hypnotic depth. The researchers have come up with all kinds of scales and tables, with degrees of depth varying from five on some, to as many as fifty on others. Some rate arm catalepsy as an indication of a light trance, while others maintain that a subject must be in a deep state to achieve it. But whatever the measurements agreed upon, they cannot affect the reality of your natural degree of suggestibility, or help you attain it.

Another obstacle on the path to the deepest trance possible is skepticism. If you don't have faith both in the potential of hypnosis and in your own capacity to take advantage of it, then the greatest hypnotist in the world won't be able to guide you to maximum susceptibility. On the other hand, don't set yourself up for a mind-bending experience. People who do are invariably disappointed. If the experience doesn't live up to their expectations, they conclude they haven't been hypnotized and that hypnosis in any form is a hoax. Until this attitude is reversed, all hope of achieving hypnotic potential in subsequent sessions is lost.

Every hypnosis candidate I encounter in my forensic and therapeutic practices is introduced to the medium by means of the Hypnotic Induction Profile. The carefully-thought-out procedure is so designed that at the end of it, the subject cannot escape from the conclusion that something unusual happened to him. He may have the typical response of deciding he wasn't hypnotized because he didn't feel an out-of-the-ordinary state of consciousness. But the decision is in direct conflict with certain reactions that he knows are beyond the realm of his normal behavior. How can he tell himself that nothing took place, in the face of the evidence of his arm drifting up, independent of his will, every time I put it back down on the chair, or the tingling and floating sensations he may have experienced? He can't. He is compelled to reassess his judgment, and think, "Hey, I must have been in a kind of altered consciousness. I guess there *is* something to this hypnosis business!" Then the adventure can begin. The subject is in a positive, receptive frame, and there is no estimating the depths he will plumb when I put him back into a trance.

If you are entertaining thoughts of undergoing hypnotherapy, or are asked to be hypnotized by an investigative unit, the knowledge you are already armed with should put your attitude at least one step ahead of the average first-time subject. Still, your chances of enjoying the fullest, most stimulating experience possible will be jeopardized if the hypnotist isn't hip to the HIP. If there is no mention of it, ask about it.

Anyone interested in being hypnotized should be aware of one final stumbling block to reaching his or her built-in capacity. Paradoxically, the impediment is trying too hard. Hypnosis is a letting-go process. You have to be relaxed enough to *allow* it to happen. The more you attempt to force the experience upon yourself, the more tension you will accumulate and the further you will be removed from your goal. In this respect, the medium is closely related to acting. The best actors don't try to *act*. They work, instead, to free themselves of tension, anxiety, self-consciousness, anything that threatens to prevent the emotion appropriate to the moment from welling up from the gut spontaneously. Grounded in this principle, the finest acting technique provides the actor with ways to create an atmosphere conducive to the unexpected, the unanticipated, the astonishing. And so it is with hypnosis. The only thing to go for is relaxation. But don't *try* to relax. This is a contradiction in terms. All you can really do is sit back, let go, give in, empty your mind. The hypnotist is there to show the way, until you learn to do it on your own.

Ironically, what you will be learning to do is simply a more intense form of a natural, spontaneous mental process you have been experiencing all your life. Most people are skeptical when I tell them that everyone slips in and out of a kind of hypnosis, without an induction process, in the course of a day. But just think about the times when you are wrapped up in a really good book, or a play or film. There are moments here and there when you become so involved with the story and the characters that you suspend objectivity and become a part of the action. You never totally lose sight of the fact that you are sitting at home or in a theater. You just set aside that reality for the time being. And nothing distracts you. There may be intense noise and activity all around, but it doesn't intrude on the private world you have created. The state of mind you are in is a curious one, a delicate interplay of heightened concentration and diminished awareness of anything outside of what you are focusing on.

You don't have to be reading or watching some form of entertainment either. You could be staring off into space or at the floor, lost in thought. These are the moments when visualizations and remembrances become more vivid, and when the subconscious seems to relinquish ideas, associations, and, in turn, is more receptive to resolutions, reassessments. This is how some people achieve such behavior modification as avoiding fattening foods or giving up cigarettes without the advantage of structured hypnotic induction. If they make aversive suggestions to themselves often enough, in these instances of daydreaming—the period just before falling asleep is another—the subconscious eventually takes the hint and begins governing their actions accordingly, without their being consciously aware of how or why their usual life patterns are changing. A certified, Grade A trance, of course, operates on a deeper, surer plane, greatly speeding up this behavioral process for these people, and making it available to those who would otherwise have no access to it.

The shroud of mysticism that has clung to hypnosis for centuries could be thrown off finally if the world would only accept the fact that a trance is as natural, harmless, and prevalent as sleeping, dreaming, laughing, loving, hoping. Until then, we will never fully understand hypnosis, or appreciate it as a potential source of betterment for all mankind.

It should at least be obvious to you at this point that, popular assumption aside, hypnosis bears little resemblance to sleep. In fact, this is one of the very few things about the phenomenon that has been confirmed scientifically; it has been determined that the electrical brain-wave patterns of the two states are decidedly different. To carry the comparison with other mental processes further, I would say that hypnosis is more akin to the inner calm, yet heightened awareness, of meditation or the Alpha-brain-wave state of biofeedback fame. Like these disciplines of the mind, a hypnotic trance appears to be a key to unlocking the brain's seemingly limitless resources. After years of investigation, we still don't know if extrasensory perception is anything more than wishful thinking. Yet many of the people who attempt various kinds of psychic phenomena do so while under a hypnotic trance. I don't know why this is, but it wouldn't unnerve me if hypnosis one day showed us the way to the brain's yet-to-be-discovered frontiers.

I do know that the endlessly fascinating discipline has shown me a wonderful way of life. Aside from the career and cause it has provided me with, I wouldn't be the calm, confident person I trust I am without frequent doses of self-hypnosis. There was a time when I would get awfully rattled over the smallest disturbance. But I learned how to go into auto-hypnosis and tell myself that the situation couldn't be as bad as I was making it. Regaining my composure became easier and easier, and now nothing bothers me. And for a member of the largest police force in the country, this is saying a great deal. In fact, I may be a little too non-reactive these days in areas that I should perhaps give a little bit more thought to. But being too laid back is far better than becoming uptight, aggravated, and annoyed at the slightest provocation.

On a more mundane level, in addition to using hypnosis as a fast energizer, as I mentioned earlier, I put it to work to help me absorb the information in the reams of investigative and hypnotic reports, bulletins, manuals, journals, and books I plow through regularly. I have always had a problem with reading retention, but hypnosis has helped me conquer it. After I have finished an article or a section of a book, I put myself under and quickly review the material. This seems to allow the information to sink in deeper and stay put far longer than it ordinarily would.

I have found the limit of my own hypnotic susceptibility, not through knowledge or training, but by being inspired to match the performance of some of the subjects I have hypnotized or have had the opportunity of observing. I am resigned to the fact that I am not the most suggestible subject in the world. There isn't much I can do about that, but my capacity seems to serve my purposes just fine. I may never be able to have surgery without anesthesia, yet my supposedly limited hypnotic capability has never let me down in anything I have called upon it to help me with.

Whether large or small, yours will do the same for you, especially if you have allowed my experiences to expand your understanding of the hypnotic process. I have the utmost confidence that you won't hesitate to seek it out to fulfill your fondest dreams, or suffer a wink of anxiety if asked to be entranced to retrieve that crucial remembrance that could put one more criminal behind bars.

What does the future hold for hypnosis? The possibilities are awesome, limited only by the imaginations of the many now involved in serious investigation of the bedazzling phenomenon. The prognosis looks good, and the one claim I can make with any degree of certainty is that this is definitely not . . . the end.

POSTSCRIPT

Shortly after the completion of this book, Sergeant Diggett retired from full-time service with the New York City Police Department. He now resides in Myrtle Beach, South Carolina,
where he maintains a hypnosis counseling service and continues
to act as a consultant in forensic hypnosis to law-enforcement
agencies in various parts of the country.